OF MEN AND MUSKETS

Stories of the Civil War

Civil War Heritage Series—Volume XI

by

Robert P. Broadwater

BURD STREET PRESS

This Burd Street Press publication
was printed by
Beidel Printing House, Inc.
63 West Burd Street
Shippensburg, PA 17257-0152 USA

In respect for the scholarship contained herein, the acid-free paper used in this book meets the guidelines for permanence and durability of the Committee on Production Guidelines for Book Longevity of the Council on Library Resources.

For a complete list of available publications
please write
Burd Street Press
Division of White Mane Publishing Company, Inc.
P.O. Box 152
Shippensburg, PA 17257-0152 USA

Library of Congress Cataloging-in-Publication Data

Broadwater, Robert P., 1950–
    Of men and muskets : stories of the Civil War / by Robert P.
Broadwater.
        p.   cm. -- (Civil War heritage series : v. 11)
    Includes bibliographical references.
    ISBN 1-57249-105-1 (alk. paper)
        1. United States--History--Civil War, 1861–1865--Biography-
-Anecdotes. 2. Generals--United States--Biography--Anecdotes.
3. Generals--Confederate States of America--Biography--Anecdotes.
I. Title. II. Series.
E467.B828   1998
973.7'092--dc21   98-7161
                                                               CIP

PRINTED IN THE UNITED STATES OF AMERICA

To my wife with love

CONTENTS

INTRODUCTION

The four tragic years of violence known as the American Civil War have produced a legacy which has been handed down from generation to generation. Given the sincerity with which the contest was waged by each side, along with the appalling number of casualties exacted upon the battlefield, one might easily believe that this legacy was one of bitterness and hatred. Quite the opposite has proven to be the case. This war, a truly American war, called forth the best that was in every citizen living within its borders. Patriotism, gallantry, and sacrifice were demanded of the people of the era as in no other period of the nation's history prior to the war, and in no period of her history since. The people caught up in this war were swept away by forces which were beyond their power to control. It was almost as if a court of nature had determined to try the resolve of the people to prove whether the American democratic system was worthy of its founders. Yet, amid these terrible times, the people of the nation, both North and South, found strength of purpose and of character to sustain themselves and their loved ones through a transition which witnessed the death of America as she had been and the birth of a new America, the America that would become a global power by the turn of the century and serve as an inspiring example of freedom to all the people of the world who sought liberty.

How is it that the nation could become involved in such a self-destructive war in the first place, and once involved, how could the rival sections make such a complete and lasting peace when it was over? The answer to both questions is that the two sections of the nation had much more in common than anyone on either side would have cared to admit prior to the conflagration. Sectional pride along with a population that was not greatly disposed towards travel beyond their own familiar surroundings produced a prejudice of ignorance towards people from other sectors of the country. Without firsthand knowledge of day-to-day life in other sections, many people formed their opinions of North or South based upon slanderous stereotypes or exaggerated editorials. Each side saw itself as the true progenitor of freedom as the forefathers intended it to be with the other side assuming the role of a spoiler who wished to destroy that liberty which was held so dear. Each side felt itself superior to the other. Each blamed the other for any difficulties it endured, and all the while, ignorance served to escalate the problem until it could be settled in no other way than to decide the matter with the blood of the nation's sons and daughters.

As the war progressed, and its price became exceedingly more terrible, Americans on either side began to realize a truth—that they had gravely underestimated the determination and stamina of their opponent. The passing of more time revealed that there was more to admire in the people who were being called an enemy than there was to denounce. It was undeniable that a bond existed between the opposing sides which was inconsistent with such a fratricidal war. This bond found its roots in the free minds of the people, a people who had fought for and cherished liberty, and a people who would rather die than relinquish that God-given right. In the end, the similarities of action and belief among the people of the country helped turn this national tragedy into a national triumph—a triumph of the spirit of the American citizen. Ample glory was afforded to all, each side sharing in the victory as well as the defeat.

The focus of this book is to give the reader an insight into the similarities of some of the great men who fought the war on either side. It is intended to show, through story and anecdote, that the men who fought in the Civil War were nothing more than normal citizens of their day and that they were all truly American. Myth and legend have surely become a part of the history of these leaders, as contemporaries sought to memorialize their deeds and accomplishments. This in no way diminishes the importance of the stories, rather, it serves to exemplify the respect and reverence these men earned through their actions. May these tales, in some small way, bring the great players of this national drama alive for you as you read about what made them laugh and cry, fight and forgive. I hope that you enjoy these stories and that you will join with me in celebrating the triumph of character which has been handed down to us by all of these founders of our modern nation.

BEFORE THE FIGHTING

POST OF DUTY

Francis Smith, commandant of the United States Military Academy at West Point, once called a cadet to his office and asked him to wait in the anteroom while he attended to other business. Smith became so engaged in this other business that he forgot all about the young cadet waiting in the other room and went home for the evening. The next morning when the commandant returned to his office, there was the cadet, still waiting in the anteroom. Smith apologized profusely for his oversight and then asked the man why he had not left and returned to his barracks once it had become obvious that his meeting with the commandant was not going to take place. "It never occurred to me to leave the spot of duty where my superior told me to stay," replied the cadet. The cadet established himself as a man of character that day with his commandant. Later, he would establish himself as a man of character with the world. His name was Thomas J. Jackson.

Lieutenant General Thomas J. "Stonewall" Jackson. A man of strong convictions, Jackson was adored in the South, and he was both feared and respected in the North.

Leib Image Archives

SOUTHERN STUDIES

General Daniel Harvey Hill started his own personal war with the North long before the first shots were fired over Sumter or the opposing armies met on the plain of Manassas. He had been a mathmatics teacher immediately prior to the outbreak of hostilities and had compiled a textbook on the subject for the instruction of his pupils. This was no ordinary textbook. This was D. H. Hill's first assault on the North, but it was pressed forward with words instead of bayonets. Problems in the book called for such calculations as the relative speeds of two Northern soldiers fleeing a Mexican War battlefield, or the profits of a Connecticut purveyor of wooden nutmegs.

BIRTHDAY CELEBRATIONS

General Ulysses S. Grant was a devoted family man and he loved to romp and play with his children. He was also not above entering into practical jokes with them. His daughter, Nellie, had been born on the Fourth of July, and for the first few years of the child's life, Grant had convinced her that the fireworks and parades which took place on Independence Day were all in celebration of her birthday.

THE WORM TURNS

Abraham Lincoln had met his future secretary of war, Edwin Stanton, long before his election as president, back in the days when he was making his living as a country attorney, riding the circuit in search of cases. He was to appear as counsel in an important case outside Illinois, in conjuction with an important lawyer from the east, Mr. Stanton. This could be Lincoln's chance to improve himself in the legal community, and a good showing would have assured that he could give up riding the circuit. None of his hopes came to pass though, for Stanton viewed this backwoods lawyer as a bumpkin and treated him with the utmost of contempt, not even allowing him to open his mouth in the courtroom. Many years later, it was Lincoln who was calling the shots, but Stanton was not to be suffered by his ungracious manner in bygone days. Lincoln admired the good qualities of the man's nature and deferred a great deal of responsibility to him.

FAMILY TIES

General Joe Johnston's wife must have given her complete support to her husband's efforts towards securing independence for the Southern Confederacy. Surely, she understood the sacrifices which would have to be made before that independence could come to pass. You see, Mrs. Johnston came from a family who was proud of their contributions in the struggle for freedom. Her most famous ancestor was another Virginian who had struggled for freedom, Patrick Henry.

A DIVERSE PERSONALITY

Lincoln's secretary of war, Edwin Stanton, was a hard-driving, dedicated man who demanded the most out of himself and was not willing to settle for anything less from anyone else. Most of the people who came in contact with him left with a feeling that they had just encountered the most obstinate, temperamental man alive. His ability to make people dislike him was only exceeded by his ability in handling the War Department. Stanton was hardly the sort of man who would lead one to believe that somewhere beneath all that efficiency, somewhere behind the image beat a heart as compassionate as any man's. As a young man, he had lost a sweetheart to death and the shock was so great to him that his grieving knew no bounds. He refused to accept the fact that she was dead, insisting that the girl had been buried alive, and could not be convinced of the fact until he had the body exhumed to examine it. Later in his life, death paid a visit to someone else he loved in the person of his young daughter. Once more his grief knew no bounds. Stanton could not bear the thought of being separated from his child, even by death, and he kept her casket in his room for some time before finally being able to part with her. These are not the acts of a man who did not have a heart, a man void of emotion. As head of the War Department, it was Stanton's responsibility to pursue the active prosecution of the war and in so doing, to assure that young men would die. It is possible that most men never met the real Edwin Stanton, instead, they met a man who was trying to deal with all of the death around him in the only way he could, pouring himself into his work and keeping the rest of the world at arm's length.

USING HIS TALENTS

In 1852, Robert E. Lee assumed the post of superintendent at the United States Military Academy at West Point. For the next three years, he was in charge of the training of many of the future generals of the Civil War. No less than two dozen future Union generals were under his tutelage at this time as well as a number of future Union commanders who were on his staff. Lee was an excellent judge of character, and some historians say that his time at West Point accounts for a large portion of his success against the Union army, as he had successfully estimated the strengths and weaknesses of his opponents through earlier contact. This is not an assumption to be taken lightly. When the Civil War began, Lee had been in the service for thirty-two years, twenty-six of them were spent in staff duty and only six were spent on the line. Of those six years on the line, he only spent three years with troops, and at no time had he ever commanded a force larger than three hundred men. So you see, Lee did not have experience in handling large bodies of men, and his battlefield exposure was limited. He owed his success more to a sharp, clear mind and an ability to correctly estimate the actions of his opponents than to practical knowledge gained from experience.

HIS BETTER HALF

General Nathan Bedford Forrest was the epitome of dash and daring in war—traits which were not uncommon to his private life as well. A story is told of how he first met the girl he would marry which serves to exemplify the point. The year was 1845, and Forrest was 24 years old. He was out on a Sunday morning ride when he happened to see a carriage stuck in the mud of a creek crossing. Two other young men were already at the scene, but they were contented to merely watch the events which transpired rather than taking an active part. Forrest lost no time in rescuing the occupants of the carriage, Miss Mary Ann Montgomery and her widowed mother, carrying them both to safety. He then waded back into the mud to extricate the ladies' carriage. Once the rescue was complete, the two young men received his attention as he chased them from the scene with threats of violence. Introducing himself to the ladies, he asked and was granted permission to call on Miss Montgomery. On visiting the Montgomery home, he found the same two men who had been at the creek already seated on the front porch. His anger over their inaction had not yet subsided, and once more he chased them off.

That day, only the second time he had ever met Mary Ann, he proposed to her. She accepted on their next meeting, but Forrest still had to receive the consent of her uncle and foster father, the Reverend Samuel Montgomery Cowan. The Reverend was an important man of God in those parts, and his opinion of the proposed marriage was less than enthusiastic.

"Why, Bedford," he said, "I couldn't consent. You cuss and gamble and Mary Ann is a Christian girl."

"I know it," Forrest replied, "and that's just why I want her."

Persistence paid off, and Bedford Forrest and Mary Ann Montgomery were married a few months later.

FAIR WARNING

General John Logan was known to his troops as a fair and honest man. Through battlefield experience he proved that he was also a capable leader of men, but in the beginning of the war the respect he was tendered by the men was the result of his high-toned ethics and his policy of fair play. This had been a trademark of Logan's ever since he had been a small boy. In fact, he first gained notoriety in his town at the age of ten when he posted a notice of warning in his family's fields telling intruders what would happen if they were caught there. The message read: "I give notice to all squirrels to keep out of this cornfield. If they don't keep out they will be shot. John A. Logan."

I'LL DO MY DUTY

"Stonewall" Jackson showed at an early age that he was not one to shirk his responsibilities, even when he had the opportunity. As a cadet at the military academy, Jackson roomed with the cadet who served as orderly sergeant and was offered immunity from morning roll calls by his roommate. Though being assured that his absence would never be reported, Jackson refused the offer and stood his place in the line every day.

STOUT OF HEART

General Nathaniel Lyon seemed destined to die, as he did at Wilson's Creek, a gallant and dashing, if not a rash, death. In the days when he was stationed at Fort Riley, before the war, he had once insulted a fellow officer on the issue of slavery and was challenged to a duel. Lyon refused the challenge at first, but he was eventually goaded by his peers into accepting. As the challenged party, Lyon had choice as to manner of combat, and he selected pistols. This was not at all uncommon, if the duel was fought in the conventional way of the combatants walking ten paces in opposite directions, then turning to fire. That was not what Lyon proposed. He chose to fight the duel from across a table, a method which was sure to be fatal to both combatants. No one doubted Lyon's resolution to go through with his plans, and the offended man's second talked him into recalling the challenge to prevent the useless death of both of them.

THE MORE THE MERRIER

"Stonewall" Jackson is not conceived to be a passionate romantic, but the honeymoon trip he planned after his marriage to Eleanor Junkin would seem to show otherwise. The happy couple went on an extensive trip which took them to New York City, Niagara Falls, Canada, Boston, and West Point. Truly, this was an elaborate, extended honeymoon for those days, and the couple had the opportunity to start their life together in the atmosphere of a long holiday. I have stated that it would seem that Jackson was a romantic under the skin, and so far, the story does not dispute this. There is, however, another part of the story which shatters this premise. The happy couple were not the only ones enjoying their honeymoon in all of the places mentioned. As a matter of fact, they enjoyed very little in private during this trip, for they had a traveling companion along, Eleanor's sister, Margaret.

STANTON'S JUSTICE

Edwin Stanton was an able and intelligent lawyer in the days before the Civil War. His specialty was corporate law but he would take a criminal case from time to time if that case seemed challenging enough and if the fee was large. The fee and the challenge seemed to be the major considerations for Stanton, not the guilt or innocence of his client. In one murder case he agreed to defend the accused man, accepting as his payment the man's only possession, his house. After the trial was over and the client had been cleared, Stanton sought to convert the mortgage on the house into cash for his payment but the client begged him not to, pleading that the foreclosure would ruin him. "You deserve to be ruined," said Stanton, "for you were guilty."

Secretary of War Edwin Stanton. Known as a cold, hard-driving superior in the War Department, Stanton had a soft side that most of his contemporaries never saw. Work seems to have been an outlet for the tragedies which had occurred in his life.

Leib Image Archives

WHAT IF?

Robert E. Lee was on duty in Texas when that state seceded from the Union. He had just received orders to travel to Washington for an interview, and while securing transportation in San Antonio, he was informed that General David Twiggs had surrendered all Federal property and troops in the state. Since he had already been detached from his service in Texas by orders to appear in Washington, Lee felt himself excluded from the surrender terms. To avoid the possibility of problems he, nonetheless, changed into civilian clothes before continuing. Texas state authorities met him at the train station and refused to allow him to board. He was a Yankee officer and a prisoner as far as they were concerned, and the only way they were going to allow him to leave was if he resigned his commission immediately in the Union army and became a Confederate officer. This, Lee refused to do. After some consideration, the Texas authorities backed down on their demands and allowed Lee to continue. The greatest hero of the South almost began the war as a prisoner of the very cause he was to uphold so nobly.

WAR! THE NATION DIVIDES

Many high appointments were made in the army for the purpose of binding the country together in support of the war. Every effort was made by the administration to ensure that no one group of people would be alienated, and each had their representation among the officer corps. In many instances the men who received these appointments were unqualified to hold such high positions, but it was hoped that the sectional support their names would lend to the cause would more than make up for their personal inadequacies. One day, while Stanton and Lincoln were discussing possible appointments for brigadier generals, Lincoln is quoted as saying, "There has got to be something done unquestionably in the interest of the Dutch, and to that end I want Schimmelfennig appointed." The name delighted Lincoln and he resisted Stanton's attempt to suggest other German-American officers that might be more qualified by stating, "No matter about that, his name will make up for any difference there may be," and off he went repeating the name over and over again.

FOLLOW US

William T. Sherman had his men positioned by the stream at Bull Run as he explored to find a ford by which they could cross. None was to be found, but the search went on until the Union troops were unknowingly shown its location by the enemy. A group of Confederate horsemen rode into the stream to yell threats at the Yankees and in so doing accomplished what Sherman's men had not, by showing the location where the stream was shallow enough to cross.

THE GOSPEL ACCORDING TO PENDLETON

It is difficult to reconcile war and religion, especially when one is a servant of God, called upon to fight for one's country. General William Pendleton must surely have had this problem when he was elected captain of the Rockbridge Artillery at the beginning of the war. Pendleton was an Episcopal rector in Lexington, Virginia. Though he had been schooled as a soldier at West Point, he had given up martial pursuits in favor of spiritual ones. When war broke out, he chose to fight for the South and the unit he joined was specially suited to his spiritual past, for the Rockbridge Artillery was chiefly composed of seminary students, and the four guns of the battery were named: Matthew, Mark, Luke and John.

WHO'S THE BOSS?

Though latent talent abounded in the officer corps of both sides at the beginning of the Civil War, no officer on either side had ever commanded the numbers of men that armies of this war would contain. For this reason, some politicians in the North entertained the idea of recruiting a proven general from abroad to lead the national armies. George Klapka, hero of the 1849 Hungarian Revolution, was one of the popular candidates for the job. Klapka's financial demands for assuming the position quickly convinced his supporters that he was not the right man for the country. Klapka stated that he would require an advance payment of $100,000 and an annual salary of $25,000. He further demanded that he be given the post of chief of staff until he had learned the English language, then made general in chief. His demands were, indeed, extreme in a day when the average American brigadier general earned only $124 a month.

WHAT DO THEY LOOK LIKE?

Photography had only recently become affordable to the masses at the outbreak of the Civil War. Everyone wished to be immortalized for all time through this amazing novelty. The Civil War, with its ability to create national heroes, gave rise to a thriving business by photographers to mass market images of the famous men of the day. One of the first instances of this occurred in Charleston, South Carolina, and oddly enough, involved the sale of pictures of Northern heroes in that city. A Charleston photographer by the name of George Crook had visited Fort Sumter during the siege but prior to the bombardment he had convinced the officers to sit for a picture. Citizens of Charleston were anxious to see what these Yankees looked like and the copies of the picture enjoyed brisk sales in the city. Thus, one of the earliest mass marketing ventures in photography, occurring in the birthplace of secession, portrayed Northern, not Southern, heroes.

CURIOUS CURSING

"Stonewall" Jackson is well known for his piety and the strength of his religious convictions. He neither swore nor imbibed of strong liquor—traits shared with Robert E. Lee and J.E.B. Stuart. In the early days of the war, before he had proven his military abilities and established himself as one of the premier soldiers ever produced on the American continent, these attributes were viewed by the men as eccentricities which substantiated the tales they had heard about their new commander's odd behavior. These were the days when "Tom Fool" was still the nickname used when talking about Jackson. On the battlefield that was to change his nickname forever, Bull Run, Jackson came as close as he ever did to swearing, and it caused his men no end of amusement. While his troops were waiting on the ridge near the Henry House, he cautioned them to be vigilant in watching for the enemy to emerge from a stand of pines. "Now men," he said, "if you see any Yankees come out of these pines, give them pepper." A chorus of laughter broke forth from the ranks at this peculiar sort of swearing, causing Jackson to turn in his saddle adding, "and salt too." "Tom Fool" was soon to be dropped as a nickname for Jackson, and his troops came to view his eccentricities as signs of genius rather than absurdity.

QUARTERMISTRESS

At the beginning of the war, when Bradley Johnson was going to Harpers Ferry to take command of his first unit, his wife decided that it was her duty to accompany him to the front and ease his privations in any way she could. Upon reaching the camp, the first thing she noticed was that his men were without weapons. At once, she took it upon herself to rectify the situation by making a trip to North Carolina to see some influential friends who could possibly raise the money with which the arms could be purchased. While in the state, she presented her case to the governor, who satisfied her request by donating five hundred .54 caliber rifled muskets, ten thousand rounds of ammunition, and three thousand five hundred musket caps. From North Carolina, Mrs. Johnson went to Richmond where she had an interview with Governor John Letcher. From him she secured blankets, tents and other camp equipage, the whole of which was delivered to her husband's command back at Harpers Ferry. With his wife around, Johnson had no need for a quartermaster officer and, as a soldier's wife, she was probably the closest to a professional that he could have found among his raw volunteers.

NOT A WALLFLOWER

As the combatants maneuvered in preparation for the Battle of Bull Run, their movements were being watched by a throng of spectators who had come down from Washington to observe the battle. There was a holiday spirit among the civilians. They brought picnic baskets and opera glasses and made plans to watch the proceedings as if it were to be a sporting event. Few of them realized that both sides were in deadly earnest and that a grim, terrible war was about to break loose in America. One of the civilians decided that there was more to be done than to simply sit and watch. He was unwilling to be a spectator when so many brave men were about to risk their lives and thus he determined to become a participant. John Logan, a congressman from Illinois at the time, sought out a Michigan regiment, which accepted his services, and volunteered to fight with it in the battle. This was the beginning of a long and brilliant military career that saw Logan rise to the rank of general officer and become a major influence in the Union army by the end of the war.

ONLY HIS HAIRDRESSER KNOWS

General Pierre G. T. Beauregard was a dashing and handsome man and was accused of vanity by some of his critics. When his black hair began to turn gray in 1861, his friends and supporters attributed it to the strains he had been under and the burden of command. His critics had altogether another explanation for the occurrence. They claimed that Beauregard had dyed his hair and the Union blockade had cut off the import of hair dyes from abroad.

WHICH WAY DO WE GO?

Rarely, if ever, are battles won by an army that adopts a retreat as its course of action. One exception, on record, is a retreat ordered by General Ambrose E. Burnside during his expedition in North Carolina. The Federal army had run up against strongly emplaced batteries at New Bern and the troops were becoming discouraged by their fire. A staff officer rode up to Burnside and asked if the general wished to order a retreat. "Retreat!" Burnside said, "Yes, right into the face of the enemy. That is how I want you to retreat."

BABY FACE

Alexander Stephens, vice president of the Confederacy, was a slight man in stature. His small, frail frame gave him a youthful, if not childish, appearance which belied the serious, thoughtful personality of the man. Once, in the beginning of the war, Stephens was riding on a train when his slight appearance caused him a bit of embarrassment. A fellow passenger mistook him for a boy and hailed him, "Sonny, get up and give your seat to the gentleman."

LIARS CLUB

An amusing story is told of an Irish volunteer who went into his colonel's office in search of a furlough. He told his commander that he needed to return home because his wife was ill and his children were not well. The colonel fixed a suspicious eye on the soldier and replied, "Pat, I had a letter from your wife this morning saying she doesn't want you at home; that you raise the devil when you are there, and that she hopes I won't grant you any more furloughs. What have you to say to that?"

The Irishman looked at him for a second and then replied that there were "two splendid liars in this room" and that he was only one of them. "I nivir was married in me life."

NAME THAT TUNE

"Dixie" quickly became a popular song of the Confederacy after the war broke out, its proud lyrics and lively rhythm having inspirational qualities for the people of the South. The song was a favorite at all types of gatherings and few people did not know the words and tune by heart. Strangely enough, "Stonewall" Jackson was among those precious few who did not recognize the Confederate anthem. Once, while he and his staff were being entertained by a bit of music in the parlor of a Southern home, Jackson asked the girl who was entertaining them, "Won't you play a piece of music they call 'Dixie'? I heard it a few days ago and thought it was beautiful."

The girl was dumbfounded and informed the general that she had just finished singing "Dixie."

"Ah, indeed," Jackson said, "I didn't know it."

ALL TIED UP

General P. G. T. Beauregard encountered much difficulty in receiving supplies for his army prior to the first Battle of Bull Run. It seemed that there was a shortage of everything: food, weapons, and ammunition. There was even a lack of rope for well buckets, and when Beauregard put in a requisition for it he was told that none could be had as the government had decreed that all rope belonged to the navy. "If they would only send us less law and more rope," Beauregard complained. "To hang ourselves with, General?" one of his staff playfully inquired. "It would be better than strangulation with red tape," Beauregard replied.

LOOK ALIKES

Company E of the 41st Tennessee, Gregg's Brigade, claimed a distinction which no other company in the Confederate army could match: it contained three sets of twins. Though it was a novelty, this situation posed a problem for the officers which can be seen by the following incident. One pair of twins, Edwin and Walter Beardon, were both lieutenants and it seems that Walter was serving as officer of the day at Port Hudson when some confusion over the identity of the brothers occurred. General John Gregg observed Edwin walking about camp with his coat unbuttoned and his sword belt unfastened. Feeling that this was no example to be set by an officer of the day, Gregg arrested Edwin for his appearance. Edwin did not protest the fact that he had been arrested because he did not know that it was due to a case of mistaken identity. Instead, he reported under arrest to the general, ready to accept whatever punishment was administered. At this moment, Walter happened to pass by in perfect military attire and the general and Edwin both realized the error which had been made. Both men laughed heartily at the mistake and Gregg dropped all charges.

WHO DO I FIGHT?

The nation was not prepared for war of the scale that the Civil War assumed when the green troops of both sides met to do battle at Bull Run. Major battles in America's previous wars would seem nothing more than minor skirmishes when compared with the engagements which were to be fought over the next four years. Indeed, the nation had a lot to learn. No one had more to learn than the men who were to fight the war. Officers who had never commanded more than a regiment of men now found themselves with the responsibility for thousands upon thousands of troops. Armies of this size had never before been assembled in America and so, there was no practical experience to draw on concerning how they should be managed. During the Battle of Bull Run, there occurred an incident which demonstrates just how difficult it was for the newly created army commanders to handle and keep track of their units. General Beauregard had issued orders to his commanders for an assault on the Union army on the morning of July 21. McDowell's Federal forces beat him to the punch by attacking first, causing tremendous confusion in the Confederate ranks. Beauregard added to this confusion by failing to cancel his own attack orders. Instead, he merely sent additional instructions to some of his commanders. His orders became so confusing that in one instance, if strictly followed, he had ordered the Confederates under General David Jones to attack the Confederates under General Richard Ewell.

General P. G. T. Beauregard. Caught up in the complex and intricate maneuvers that epitomized Napoleonic tactics, Beauregard once issued battle orders that, if strictly obeyed, would have directed one Confederate unit to attack another.

AND THE WINNER IS . . .

General Ulysses S. Grant was not considered by anyone to assume the role of a major player in the national drama of the Civil War in its early days. He had proven himself a solid soldier in his pre-war service but he seemed lacking in command ability. Then there was the matter of his alleged drinking problem. The old army had contained a rather small officer corps, and the accomplishments and habits of any officer were well known to all. Rightly or wrongly, Grant had been labeled as a drunkard in the old army, and the issue was constantly revived whenever he was discussed by contemporaries. Indeed, his prospects for advancing to high station in the beginning of the war seemed bleak. He might very well have served throughout the conflict as an obscure brigade or division commander if fate had not stepped in and pushed him to the forefront.

It seems that General John "Pathfinder" Frémont was conducting a council of war to determine what was to be done to protect the Ohio River region after the Confederate army, under Leonidas Polk, had invaded the state of Kentucky. One of the topics of discussion was who would be named as commander of the Federal forces in western Kentucky. Many names were bantered about, but a selection was not made. General Justus McKinstry, a member of Frémont's staff, had entered the meeting late. On his way through the building, he had passed by General Grant, a newly commissioned brigadier, and had stopped briefly to exchange pleasantries. Grant was waiting to see Frémont for the purpose of being reprimanded for the conduct of his command.

McKinstry, at length, tired of the arguing about who should get the command, and he suggested to Frémont: "Oh, give it to Grant downstairs there." Frémont did, and the rest is history.

THE NATION LEARNS HOW TO FIGHT

HABITUALLY HOOKED

The familiar picture of General Ulysses S. Grant is an average-sized man with a close cropped beard, clothes a bit on the unkempt side, a slouch hat pulled down low on his forehead, and a cigar protruding from his mouth. In fact, cigars have become almost as much a part of the Grant legend as the controversial allegations of the general's drinking excesses. Grant had been only an occasional smoker before the war. In his own words, he tells of how he acquired the habit. "I had been a very light smoker previous to the attack on Donelson, and after that battle I acquired a fondness for cigars by reason of a purely accidental circumstance. Admiral Foote, commanding the fleet of gunboats which were cooperating with the army, had been wounded, and at his request, I had gone aboard his flagship to confer with him. The admiral offered me a cigar, which I smoked on my way back to my headquarters. On the road I was met by a staff officer, who announced that the enemy was making a vigorous attack. I galloped forward at once, and while riding among the troops giving directions for repulsing the assault I carried the cigar in my hand. It had gone out, but it seems that I continued to hold the stump between my fingers throughout the battle. In the accounts published in the papers I was represented as smoking a cigar in the midst of the conflict; and many persons, thinking, no doubt, that tobacco was my chief solace, sent me boxes of the choicest brands from everywhere in the North. As many as ten thousand were soon received. I gave away all I could get rid of, but having such a quantity on hand, I naturally smoked more than I would have done under ordinary circumstances, and I have continued the habit ever since."

Lieutenant General Ulysses S. Grant. While enjoying little "luck" in civilian life, Grant received a stroke of good fortune in obtaining his first important field command when he just happened to be in the right place at the right time.

A GAME OF CHANCE

Nathan Bedford Forrest had been an avid gambler before the war, and his opponents in blue would have been wise to have remembered that when they fought against him. On more than one occasion, Forrest resorted to bluffing his adversary into folding what would have been a military advantage. His first attempt at this took place at Murfreesboro, Tennessee in the summer of 1862 when he led his cavalry in a surprise attack against a strong garrison located in the town. Forrest's troops made quick work of a Union force on the eastern side of the town which was captured when Forrest demanded their surrender "to prevent the effusion of blood." He then turned his full attention to a portion of the garrison located on the western side of the town, demanding their surrender as well. This unit was led by a commander who was not as easily convinced that the fight was over, and he stayed in the game a little longer by asking to meet with the commander of the captured Yankee force to ascertain that he had, indeed, surrendered. Forrest agreed and the Union officer was escorted to the place where the prisoners were being held. Along the way, he was greeted with the sight of Confederate troopers coming and going through the streets of the town in staggering number. Obviously, Forrest did, indeed, have an overpowering force and the Federal officer determined that if he had been left to fight it alone, he had better surrender. What he did not know was that the Confederate troopers he had seen in the streets of the town had been putting on a show in his honor. Forrest had shifted his force back and forth through the streets of Murfreesboro, and the Federal officer had seen the same men many times on his way to the meeting, calculating them to be different parts of a vastly superior force. Forrest had played his bluff to the limit and in the end, the Union forces surrendered the game to the gambler.

GIVING THE SLIP

General P. G. T. Beauregard was caught in a trap at Corinth, Mississippi by a vastly superior Union force under the command of General Henry Halleck. If he tried to hold the town he would be crushed by the weight of Halleck's forces and if he tried to retreat, his army would be broken on the move. With no good choices available, Beauregard decided to stake the future of his army on a bluff. He arranged for locomotives to be run into the town at regular intervals to be greeted each time by wild cheering from the troops. Halleck's army took the bait and the Union general was sure that the Confederates were receiving heavy reinforcements. Instead of mounting an assault, the Union army stopped and held its position to await further developments. In the meantime, Beauregard was busy shipping his army out of town to a safer place where they could refit and reorganize.

Lieutenant General Nathan Bedford Forrest. The "Wizard of the Saddle," Forrest is acknowledged as being the greatest natural military talent that the war produced. Hard-hitting attacks, mobility, and deception were all part of the tactical arsenal he used against his adversaries.

I WON'T TELL IF YOU DON'T

"Stonewall" Jackson rarely revealed his plans to subordinates, a circumstance which often led to complaints from the officers serving under him. It is indisputable, however, that Jackson's habit of keeping his own counsel goes far towards explaining his success. Information leaks were unheard of in Jackson's command, not because his men talked any less than their peers in other units, but because they were never given any information to talk about.

A citizen of Lexington got to learn of Jackson's closed mouth policy first hand during the Valley Campaign in 1862. He had been sent, selected by some of the town's prominent citizens, to speak with the general and inquire about his intended line of march. After Jackson had learned the purpose of the man's visit, he said, "Judge B——, can you keep a secret?"

"Most certainly," the judge assured him.

"So can I," said Jackson, concluding the interview on that note.

AN INTERRUPTION

It was the custom of the day that most officials, be they military or civilian, were not too hard for an average person to see. Lincoln spent a great deal of his time in interviews with people who were trying to get a political favor, seeking his intervention in a matter of personal interest, or trying to get his backing for a new invention for the military. So great was the public burden upon him that it is hard to imagine how he found time to run the affairs of state in the midst of a terrible Civil War. This same scenario was played over and over again by most of the leaders, both North and South. Once, an observer noted a caller who stopped in to pay his respects to General Grant. "I hain't got no business with you, General," he said, "but I just wanted to have a little talk with you, because folks will ask me if I did."

CAN'T BE DONE

Basil Duke was a lieutenant of cavalry, serving under John H. Morgan at the Battle of Shiloh. He had been ordered to charge a Union battery in the Hornet's Nest and, having a trooper among his ranks who had served with the artillery for awhile, he sought the soldier out to ask his advice.

"Good Lord, Lieutenant!" the soldier exclaimed, "I wouldn't do it if I was you. Why your blamed little cavalry won't be deuce high agin' them guns!"

Duke informed the man that he wasn't interested in his opinion. The charge on the battery was going to take place and he was only interested in finding out the best way to go about it. Looking Duke square in the eye, the soldier said, "Lieutenant, to tell you the God's truth, thar' ain't no good way to charge a battery!"

I'M NOT DRUNK

One night, while riding to headquarters with his staff, "Stonewall" Jackson fell asleep in the saddle. This was hardly the first time it had happened, and, in fact, it had become so regular an occurrence that Jackson and Dr. McGuire, of his staff, had made a pact between them to hold each other's coattails when one of them was asleep. As Jackson rode down the road, swaying in his saddle, the group passed the campfire of some stragglers. One of the stragglers, not recognizing Jackson, yelled out, "Hello! I say, old fellow, where the devil did you get your likker?"

Jackson was startled awake by the outburst. He halted his horse and asked, "Dr. McGuire, did you speak to me? Captain Pendleton, did you? Somebody did."

By this time, the straggler realized who he had been talking to and with a "Good God, it's Old Jack!" he ran away into the darkness. The staff was greatly amused by the incident, as was Jackson once they explained what had happened.

KNOW YOUR ENEMY

There was an understanding and a fellowship among the officers of the Union and Confederate armies which had not existed in any American war previously, and was not duplicated in any war which followed. Most of the officers, on both sides, had been friends and acquaintances in the old army. It would seem to follow, therefore, that the officers who served in the Civil War knew the strengths and weaknesses, the habits and idiosyncrasies of the opponents they faced more than in any other war that has ever been fought. General Richard Ewell gave emphasis to this point when he was asked his opinion of the Federal commanders by General Robert E. Lee.

"Of McDowell not highly," Ewell replied. "I do not know this McClellan; he is a younger man. But there is one West Pointer, I think in Missouri, little known, whom I hope the Northern people will not find out about. I mean Sam Grant. I should fear him more than any of their leaders I have yet heard of."

ANIMAL LOVER

General Grant was a great lover of horses. He had learned to ride at an early age and had become an excellent horseman. His affection for horses caused Grant to be an animal lover and he could not abide cruelty to any creature. Once, he happened upon a teamster who was beating a mule. Grant ordered that the man be strung up by his thumbs as punishment for the act. As he said, "I could defend myself; the poor dumb animal could say or do nothing for its own protection."

AGONY AND ECSTASY

The maiden voyage of the Confederate ironclad *Virginia* changed forever the precepts of naval warfare throughout the world. The manner in which the Confederate vessel easily disposed of her wooden adversaries, sustaining only the slightest of damage to itself, was the beginning of the end for wooden warships. It was, indeed, a big day for the Confederacy as well as for Franklin Buchanan, captain of the *Virginia*. His ship had struck fear into the national government as well as the men who served on the wooden ships who would be expected to meet the *Virginia*. All was not glory and exultation for Buchanan, however, for a heavy price was exacted for his victory. His brother, Thomas McKean Buchanan had stayed with the Union navy and was serving aboard the *Congress* when that vessel met the *Virginia*. He, however, survived the battle, only to be killed by a sniper's bullet on January 14, 1863, as commander of the gunboat USS *Calhoun* in Louisiana's Bayou Teche, when the *Congress* caught fire in its fight with his brother's ship.

OLD TIMES

Jeb Stuart met an old friend of his, under a flag of truce, during an engagement near Washington. The friend was General George Bayard, of the Union army, an old comrade who had served in the same company with Stuart before the war. In those days, Stuart was a second lieutenant and Bayard was a grade ahead of him as a first lieutenant. Now, though in different armies, the tables were turned. Stuart was the ranking officer with the grade of major general, a step above the brigadier level of his old friend. As the two stood talking, Bayard happened to hear a wounded Federal soldier cry out for a drink of water.

"Here, Jeb," he said as he tossed his bridle to the Confederate chieftain, "hold my horse a minute, will you, till I fetch that poor fellow some water." When the Union general returned from his mission of mercy, he mounted his horse, and the two men prepared to depart for their respective lines. Stuart playfully teased Bayard that it had been some time since he had "played orderly to a Union general."

ARE YOU A RINGMASTER?

It was not a good idea for an officer to have too many embellishments of rank on his uniform and mark himself as a target. Still, many officers could not resist the urge to dress up their uniforms so that they bore witness to the high rank of their wearers. One such officer was General Joseph Bartlett, and he had his uniform adorned with brilliant gold lace. Bartlett's flair was dashing but it didn't impress his more level-minded superior, General Charles Griffin, who remarked once upon seeing him, "Well, Bartlett, when will the rest of the circus arrive?"

DO AS I DO

General William T. Sherman, in the summer of 1861, observed the men of the 79th New York hiding behind trees during a period of shelling and decided to set an example for them. Riding among the troops, he cooly explained that it was no use to duck or hide. The shells the men could hear were already past by the time they became audible, he said, and you could not hear the ones headed for you anyway. The men listened as he talked but they were not convinced. Just then, a large shell hit in the trees directly over Sherman's head, creating a terrible noise. Instinctively, Sherman ducked down low on his horse's neck and when he rose again it was to see the many grinning faces of the men he had just been lecturing. Knowing that the joke was on him, he broke into a big smile and said, "Well boys, you may dodge the big ones."

HEATED WORDS

Nathan Bedford Forrest and Earl Van Dorn were once involved in an altercation caused when one of Forrest's staff officers submitted a story to a newspaper which gave credit for one of Van Dorn's victories to Forrest. Van Dorn was greatly agitated by the incident and "without mincing matters, I called his attention to the reports I had heard, and accused him of misrepresentation at headquarters. This he warmly denied and expressed his conviction of my too great willingness to listen to stories to his discredit. One thing led to another, until at length I threw off all restraint and directly expressing my belief in his treachery and falsehood, suggested that then and there was as good a time and place to settle our difficulties as any, and suiting the action to the word, I stepped to where my sword was hanging against the wall, snatched it down and turned to face him."

"Forrest was really a sight to see. He had risen and advanced one step, his sword half drawn from its scabbard, and his face aflame with feeling. But even as I unsheathed my own sword and advanced to meet him, a wave of some kind seemed to pass over his countenance; he slowly returned his sword to its sheath, and steadily regarding me said, 'General Van Dorn, you know I'm not afraid of you—but I will not fight you—and leave you to reconcile with yourself the gross wrongs you have done me. It would never do for two officers of our rank to set such an example to the troops, and I remember, if you forget, what we both owe to the cause.'" "I never felt so ashamed of myself in my life," Van Dorn said, "and recalled by Forrest's Manly [sic] attitude and words to our true position, I immediately replied that he was right, and apologized for having used such expressions to him. And so we parted to be somewhat better friends, I believe, than we had been before. Whatever else he may be, the man certainly is no coward."

UNEXPECTED AID

In the days before the Battle of Shiloh, General P. G. T. Beauregard made an appeal to the people of the Mississippi Valley to donate their plantation bells to the army so that cannon could be made from them. He stressed the fact that the cannon would be needed to protect the homes of these same plantation owners but very few donations were received from this quarter. Beauregard did end up with a surplus of brass with which to cast cannon but it came from more unlikely sources. Many churches in the region donated their church bells to the cause. In addition, enthusiasm among the women of the area was so great that many of them were giving up their brass candlesticks and andirons. Beauregard had appealed to men of war for aide, men who had supported the split with the Federal government, but he received the aid from men of peace and the devoted women of the South.

MATHEMATICALLY SPEAKING

Abraham Lincoln was talking with a guest in the White House one day about war matters when the guest asked Lincoln how large he estimated the Confederate army to be.

"About 1,200,000 men," Lincoln stated.

"Is it possible that it is that large?" asked the guest, dumbfounded by the sober manner in which Lincoln had given the answer but not able to believe that the South could field such an army.

"Well, whenever one of our generals is licked he says that he was outnumbered three or four to one," said the president, "and we have 400,000 men."

TELL 'EM WHAT YOU KNOW

"Stonewall" Jackson had a habit of not disclosing any information concerning his military plans. What with the near impossibility of preventing leaks of information during the Civil War, this was a good policy, but it often led to comical situations with the troops who never knew when or where they were going.

Jackson met a soldier in his command one day in a place where he should not have been and inquired of him, "What are you doing here?"

"I don't know," replied the soldier.

"Where do you come from?" Jackson asked.

"I don't know," the soldier again responded.

When asked to explain the meaning of his ignorance, the soldier said, "Orders were that we shouldn't know anything till after the next fight." At this, Jackson laughed and passed on.

PLAY IT AGAIN

Napoleon had a great influence on the leaders of the Civil War. He was generally considered to be the greatest military mind that had lived in the recent era, and his campaigns were studied as models of how to handle an army. Officers who showed promise were referred to as little Napoleons. It was not unreasonable, therefore, that Napoleon's battle plans should be used as guides by generals on both sides. General Beauregard was an avid student of the Frenchman's campaigns and he used the great general's plans for one of his more famous campaigns as a model for the Battle of Shiloh. Beauregard must have figured that the second time would be the charm for these plans, for the battle he used as a guide was Waterloo.

FACE FORWARD

In General John Pope's controversial speech upon taking command of the Union forces designated the Army of Virginia, he stated that, in the western armies, he was accustomed to seeing the backs of the Confederates. Not only did this statement bring forth resentment from his troops who thought that their courage was being questioned, but it also gave Confederate General Richard Ewell an opportunity to make a joke at Pope's expense. When Ewell heard the contents of Pope's statement, he was reported to have replied, "By God, he'll never see the backs of my men. Their pants are out at the rear and the sight would paralyze his western bully."

A POSITIVE ATTITUDE

After the Union victory at Shiloh, General Don Carlos Buell, in a friendly way, began to criticize General U. S. Grant for fighting a battle with the Tennessee River at his back.

"Where, if beaten, could you have retreated, General?" asked Buell.

"I didn't mean to be beaten," was Grant's reply.

"But suppose you had been defeated, despite all your exertions?" Buell pressed.

"Well," said Grant, "there were the transports to carry the remains of the command across the river."

"But, General," Buell persisted, "your whole transports could not contain over ten thousand men; and it would be impossible for them to make more than one trip in the face of the enemy."

"Well, if I had been beaten," Grant said, pausing to light a cigar, "transportation for ten thousand men would have been abundant for all that would be left of us."

Accounting for the fact that Grant had about forty-two thousand men in his army, it is obvious that he intended to sustain heavy losses before yielding the field. Is it any wonder that President Lincoln once remarked that he, "can not [sic] lose this man, he fights."

TAKE A NUMBER

General Daniel Harvey Hill considered himself an infantryman, first and foremost. He had an aversion to other branches of the service, and his sarcastic nature would be in evidence when any opportunity to make light of the other services presented itself. When he received a request for a furlough from a bandsman under his command, Hill showed his preference for the infantry by endorsing it, "Respectfully forwarded disapproved— shooters before tooters."

A WILL TO LIVE

Major Robert Wheat, the commander of the famed Louisiana Tigers, was seriously wounded at First Bull Run but he did not allow the severity of the wound to hamper his optimism about making further contributions for the Confederate effort. Shot through both lungs, his doctor sadly informed him that "there is no instance on record of recovery from such a wound." Wheat boastfully replied, "I will put my case on record." Put it on record he did, for he not only recovered, but did so rapidly and was soon back in command of his battalion.

FAIR PLAY

In 1862, Colonel John Wilder commanded a Union force of approximately 4,000 men at Munfordville, Kentucky. His job was to guard the railroad leading to Louisville, especially the bridge which crossed the Green River at that point. Wilder was not a military man. Until recently, he had been a businessman, but when Braxton Bragg's Kentucky Campaign brought him in contact with Confederate forces for the first time, he was forced to fight. In the beginning of the engagement the Union forces had everything their own way as they repulsed two attacks made by advance portions of Bragg's army. Then, Bragg brought forward his main force, surrounded the position, and sent Wilder a message, telling him that his case was hopeless and demanded his surrender. That night, a Union officer came through the lines with a flag of truce, asking to talk with General Simon B. Buckner. The officer turned out to be Wilder. He explained to Buckner that he had come to get advice, as he was not a military man and did not know what he should do under the circumstances. He told Buckner that he knew he was not only a professional soldier but an honest gentleman as well, and he wished the Confederate to tell him if, under the rules of the game, it was his duty to surrender or fight it out.

Buckner was taken aback by the frank and earnest way in which Wilder addressed him and he later said that he "would not have deceived that man under those circumstances for anything." He told the colonel that he would have to make his own decision based on what was best for his cause. Buckner pointed out that Bragg had enough artillery ringed around his position to destroy the fort in very short order, but he also said that if Wilder could aid his cause in some other place by sacrificing the men he now commanded, then it was his duty to fight to the end. After their discussion, Buckner took him to see General Bragg. While Bragg was not as cordial to Wilder as Buckner had been, he did allow the colonel to count the number of cannon he had in line to use against him. As Wilder counted, he realized that the game was up and surrendered his position. This citizen soldier had gone to his enemies for advice, and all things considered, had been dealt with quite fairly.

FEE, FIE, FOE, FUM

Longstreet's wing of the Army of Northern Virginia was quick time marching to join the hard-pressed men of Jackson's wing on the old Bull Run battlefield when one of the units received a message, purported to be from General Longstreet, that it halt. The officer in command of the unit saw Longstreet approaching, just as he was receiving the message, and he detained the messenger while he talked to the general.

"Why have you halted, sir?" an angry Longstreet inquired.

"By your order, sir," replied the officer.

"Who delivered the order?" asked Longstreet.

"That officer on the sorrel horse," was the response.

"Who authorized you to deliver the order, sir?" demanded the general of the messenger.

"General Longstreet," he immediately replied, looking the general full in the face.

"Do you know General Longstreet?" he was asked.

"I do, sir," the messenger responded, falling deeper into the trap.

"Is he present?" Longstreet asked.

"He is not, sir," the messenger answered.

"Arrest that man," Longstreet ordered to the commander of his bodyguard, "then carry him to that tree over yonder and hang him—he is a spy."

The unknown messenger acknowledged that he was, indeed, a Federal officer. He had been playing for big stakes in this game of war, and now that he was discovered, he was ready to pay a big penalty. He was hung, according to Longstreet's order, asking for neither a trial nor mercy. The Federal had paid the ultimate price for error, and General Longstreet had prevented his force from being delayed in assisting Jackson's hard-pressed veterans.

THE ILLS OF LIQUOR

Confederate soldiers enjoyed many comforts due to captured Federal supplies as the Union army made its retrograde movement down the peninsula during the Seven Days' Battle. Unfortunately, one of the troops most prized captures was a stock of liquor the Federals had left behind in their quartermaster stores. Before some officers knew it, many members of their commands had become quite drunk. The officers knew that they had to dispose of the liquor, and this was accomplished in a variety of methods, before it caused too much confusion in the ranks. Colonel Fitzhugh Lee came up with an approach which was possibly the most effective. Lee spread the rumor that the liquor had been poisoned by the Yankees before they evacuated. His ruse worked wonderfully, and as one Confederate officer noted, "bottles of champagne and beer and whiskey...sailing through the air, exploding as they fell like little bomb—shells; while the expression of agony on the tipsy faces of those who had indulged too freely, as they held their hands to their stomachs, was ludicrous in the extreme."

JACKSON AND THE FARMER

General Jackson issued orders to the men of his corps not to stray from the roads, during a march, to walk in planted fields. The crops would be needed by the men later, and it would not do to have them ruined by carelessness now. One day, when Jackson was in a hurry to get to his headquarters, the road was filled with wagon trains, and as hard as he tried to weave in and out of them, the wagons kept his progress at a snail's pace. Eyeing the fields in silence, he decided that he must violate his own orders if he was to make any headway at all. Instructing his staff to ride in single file behind him, he forged ahead into the field of tall, ripened oats. A few hundred yards ahead of the place where Jackson had entered the field stood the house where the farmer resided. A plump little man, he was sitting on his front porch reading a newspaper, and watching to make sure that his crops were not violated. Seeing the mounted party advancing through the grain, he threw down the paper and charged towards them. His face flushed red with rage, and for a time he could not overcome his anger to speak. Jackson drew in his reins before the man, and sat there ready to take his punishment like a boy who had been caught in the apple orchard. At length, the man regained enough composure to demand an explanation for the outrage.

"What in Hell are you riding over my oats for?" he bellowed. "Don't you know it's against orders?"

Jackson fingered his bridle and began to explain, but before he could get a word out the man flew into him again. "Damn it! Don't you know it's against orders? I intend to have every damned one of you arrested! What's your name anyhow?"

"My name is Jackson," responded the general.

"Jackson! Jackson!" screamed the man. "Jackson, I intend to report every one of you and have you every one arrested. Yes, I'd report you if you were old Stonewall himself instead of a set of damned quartermasters and commissaries riding through my oats! Yes, I'll report you to Stonewall Jackson myself, that's what I'll do!"

"They call me that name sometimes," said Jackson, almost as if he was half ashamed to be admitting it.

"What name?" demanded the man.

"Stonewall," Jackson answered.

"You don't mean to say you are Stonewall Jackson, do you?" the farmer asked, his anger subsiding.

"Yes, sir, I am," was the response.

The rage and contempt that had so recently been vented upon Jackson disappeared at once. In its place came a look of admiration and respect. The red had gone from his face, and tears were in his eyes as he began to wave a bandana above his head shouting, "Hurrah for Stonewall Jackson! By God, General, please do me the honor to ride all over my damned old oats!"

Once again, however, he refused to let the party pass. This time it was because he wanted an opportunity to show his hospitality, though. He offered Jackson every variety of spirit for refreshment, all of them being declined by the general. Finally, he talked Stonewall into taking a glass of cold buttermilk with him. As Jackson drank the milk, he was treated to another round of blustering oaths, only this time they sang the praises of the man who was so recently being threatened with arrest.

POSTAGE DUE

Everyone has at some time or another complained about the slowness of the mail service, whether that slowness is real or imagined. General Lew Wallace had just cause to lodge such a complaint. Wallace had received information that General Albert Sidney Johnston had advanced from his base at Corinth, Mississippi and was heading straight for Grant's army at Pittsburg Landing. Wallace wrote out a message to Grant, and dispatched his favorite orderly to see that it was delivered. According to his instructions, the orderly was to place the dispatch in Grant's hands personally if he was still present at Pittsburg Landing. If Grant had left that place for his headquarters down river at Savannah, he was to give the message to the army postmaster to be delivered in the morning. Arriving at the landing, the orderly found that Grant had already left, so as per his instructions, he turned his valuable information over to the postal service, and went back to his camp. That was the last that was seen of the dispatch. Grant never received it, and consequently, the main body of the Union army had no inclination that the Confederate forces were in the vicinity until Johnston launched his surprise attack which opened the Battle of Shiloh.

HERE'S TO YOU

Ben Butler became one of the most hated men in the South during the war because of his strict enforcement of martial law during his tenure as military commander at New Orleans. His actions, though comparatively mild by modern-day standards, were considered an outrage during this romantic period, and he was pronounced to be a scoundrel and a beast throughout the Confederacy. A method was found, however, by which the citizens of New Orleans could show their utter contempt for him without doing so in public and subjecting themselves to the military punishment that would surely follow. In fact, this act of contempt, by nature, was one that could only be done in private. It seems that someone came up with the idea of placing a picture of the good general on the inside of an article of toiletry known as a night vase. These vases soon became a novelty fad in the city and Butler was saluted, in a fashion, nightly by a great many of the citizens. Indeed, Butler made such a negative impression upon the inhabitants of New Orleans that these vases remained a popular curio in the city for years after he had been transferred away.

THE COWARDS LIVE

Many stories of the Civil War evoke a feeling that this was the last of the romantic wars that the world would ever see. The codes of honor and warfare which were observed in this struggle were more akin to the knights of the round table than to modern-day war as we know it. But men like Sherman and Grant were emerging during this period and their ideas on how war should be fought were to serve as the foundation for all the modern wars that were to follow. "Stonewall" Jackson was another general who saw that war was changing, becoming more brutal than it had been before, and he adapted to this reality as can be seen by a story that is told about a meeting between him and General Richard Ewell. Jackson had heard about a courageous Federal officer who had gallantly placed himself in harm's way to urge his troops to greater effort during the Battle of Port Republic. General Ewell was said to be so taken with this show of gallantry that he went down his lines, directing his own men not to shoot at the officer. Jackson asked Ewell if the story was true, and being answered affirmatively, unleashed a storm of wrath upon his able lieutenant. "Never do such a thing again, Ewell," Jackson raged. "This is no ordinary war. The brave Federal officers are the very kind that must be killed. Shoot the brave officers and the cowards will run away and take their men with them."

STOP THE MUSIC

Fife and drum corps were an integral part of many Union regiments throughout the war, though their abundance lessened after the first couple of years. In the beginning of the war, they seemed to be everywhere, leading the trooops in one giant martial, musical parade. Colonel Adelbert Ames had just recently taken over command of the 20th Maine and was trying to form up the regiment when a fife and drum corps, of questionable training, suddenly decided to start playing. The racket was deafening and Ames could not make his orders heard over the din, so he yelled to the company commander nearest him, "Captain Bangs, stop that damned drumming!" Bangs did not respond because he could not hear the order, leaving Ames to take matters into his own hands. Drawing his sword, he charged the musicians in a one-man attack, startling and scattering the corps sufficiently to make himself once more audible to his men.

CARNAGE TO SHOCK THE NATION

THE FATHERLY TOUCH

The tough, stern reputation that "Stonewall" Jackson acquired among the troops he led was completely out of place when it came to his dealings with children. Jackson's catering ways towards the little ones never failed to win him their love and admiration. While the Southern army was camped around the city of Fredericksburg, Jackson received a splendid new uniform as a gift. The cap was especially ornate and was encircled with an elegant band of gold braid. When he appeared in camp, donning his new clothes, he noticed a young girl, of whom he was particularly fond, staring at the braid on his cap. Jackson seated himself and called the child to him. Taking her on his knee, he tore the braid off his cap and tied it around her curls, sending her on her way as the most delighted child in the city.

KEEPING UP WITH THE JONESES

The Confederacy entered the war lacking in the industrial capacity to equip a large army and keep it in the field. The army was, therefore, compelled to look for other sources to augment the munitions and supplies its factories could produce. One of the army's favorite methods of obtaining war material was to capture it from the Yankees. So successful were Confederate efforts in this field that the South was able to maintain itself moderately well with Northern goods. One North Carolina soldier, who was captured at the Battle of Antietam, was marched past a line of parked artillery, and as he passed by each piece, he read aloud the letters "U.S." stamped on the muzzles of the barrels. "Well, what now, Johnny Reb?" asked one of his captors. "I swear, Mister," he said, "you all has got most as many of these here U.S. guns as we'uns has."

HEED AND BEWARE

The Civil War era was richly steeped in romance and chivalry. The image of the Christian soldier, fighting according to a strictly enforced code of honor, was one which was deeply ingrained in the public mind. This was the last war conducted along these guidelines of "civilized" warfare, the last in which honor and dignity were more important than winning. A story is told of how General Nathan Bedford Forrest, while on a reconnaissance in the Harpeth Valley in Tennessee, observed a flag being waved by the Federal garrison in Franklin. Taking the flag to be a flag of truce, Forrest sent his own flag of truce towards the Federal line, following it closely to within pistol range of the Yankee position. At this point, a Federal officer stood up from behind a hedge and sounded a warning. "General Forrest!" he cried. "That isn't a flag of truce. It's a signal flag. Go back, sir, go back!" Forrest raised his hat to the officer in courteous response to his warning, then turned and rode away from the position as quickly as possible, expecting to be fired upon at any moment by some Federal soldier who had a less knightly concept of warfare than the officer who had issued the warning.

A VISIBLE TRAIL

When President Jefferson Davis visited the Chickamauga Battlefield shortly after the fighting there, he was taken on a tour of the ground General A. P. Stewart's division had carried in its attack. The president came upon a horse that had been killed in the battle whose trappings gave testimony to the fact that it had been a general's mount. Davis inquired as to the owner of the horse and was informed that it was Brigadier General William Bate's mount. Riding on, the president saw another dead horse about three hundred yards farther. He once again asked to whom the horse belonged and was told that it had been Bate's second mount. When the party reached the breastworks that had been held by the Federals during the battle, Davis noticed yet a third horse, lying dead upon the earthworks. This horse, too, had belonged to General Bate. Davis was duly impressed with the obvious courage Bate had shown in advancing so far in the midst of fire which was terrible enough to kill three mounts out from under him, so impressed that he had him promoted to major general soon after he got back to Richmond, even though Bate was the junior brigadier of the army.

THE ALL-STAR TEAM

Abner Doubleday, Union Civil War general and hero of Fort Sumter, was credited erroneously for decades as being the inventor of the game of baseball. Professiona teams began to spring up during the war with players receiving a portion of the gate receipts. One team, the St. Louis Empire Club, sought to increase its gate receipts by publicizing a superstar attraction as a member of the lineup. This superstar did not actually play for the team; he was merely used as a publicity stunt. His name was William T. Sherman, the first major drawing card for professional baseball.

A PRIVATE TRUCE

The Union and Confederate pickets at the base of Lookout Mountain established an informal truce between themselves which made their duty almost pleasant. Soldiers from both sides would wade in the shallow sections of Lookout Creek to trade newspapers, canteens, tobacco and coffee. This arrangement worked only when there were no officers present though, as the officers frowned upon such fraternization. A story is told of how one Union officer sided with the men and kept the truce. He had gone to a spring which both sides used for water and there met a private who was quenching his thirst. The private was dressed in blue and the officer inquired as to his unit, being told that he was one of Longstreet's men. The fact that the private was a Confederate did not startle the officer, and the two had a pleasant little chat before going their separate ways. The name of the Confederate private was not recorded, but the Union officer who kept the truce was none other than the commanding general, Ulysses S. Grant.

AN OATH OF LOYALTY

General William Rosecrans once attempted to check the Confederate ardor of some ladies of Nashville by requiring them to take an oath of loyalty to the Union. At an appointed time, they were brought into his presence, but one of the group proved obstinate in her refusal to comply with the general's wishes. She said that her mother had taught her that it was not ladylike to swear and that, because of this teaching, she could or would not take an oath. Rosecrans insisted that she must swear her allegiance or she would not be allowed to leave his presence. "Well, General," she said, "if I must swear, I will; but all sins of the oath must rest on your shoulders, for I swear on your compulsion: God damn every Yankee to hell!" With that said, this woman of the South turned and walked out of the room unmolested. I guess that even though she had not exactly taken the oath Rosecrans expected, the general's demand for an oath had been satisfied.

LOOSE FIT

General Henry Heth is known as being the general who opened the Battle of Gettysburg while looking for shoes for his men. It is interesting that Heth opened the battle due to a search for proper clothes and that his life was saved in that same battle because he did not have proper clothing himself. The hat which Heth was wearing was many times too large for his head and he had made the hat fit by folding up a newspaper and putting it on the inside of the hat, around the band. Later, when Heth was struck in the head by a minié ball, the bullet followed the course of the paper band and glanced off. Though wounded, Heth had escaped being killed by wearing a hat that was not his size.

TWO OF A KIND

Normally, there is a certain amount of professional jealousy apparent when officers from different branches of the service are placed together. This is only natural, and a healthy outgrowth of the pride an officer feels for his own branch, but this pride can sometimes stand in the way of the mutual good if it becomes petty and self-satisfying. This was not the case when William T. Sherman and David D. Porter were paired together for a combined action during the Vicksburg Campaign. The two took an instant liking to one another and formed a bond of mutual admiration and respect. When Porter was ordered to take some of his gunboats and explore Deer Creek for a possible route around the Confederate garrison at Vicksburg, Sherman and his troops were sent along as a protective force to ensure the Confederates did not block up the small river and capture the vessels. The navy had rough going in the overgrown stream, and the progress of the ships was hampered by the work of cavalry who felled trees in their path. As slow as was their progress, that of the army was even more so as the troops fought their way through the jungle of growth that surrounded the banks of the river. As a result, the navy outdistanced its protective guard, leaving it many miles to the rear. With the sound of Confederate axes at work in front of him, Porter realized that if his ships were to be trapped and attacked this would be an inviting time for the Confederates to do so. Porter was not the only one to see the potential of the situation. All of the sailors were uneasy as they looked about them at the ships that had already been battered in their fights with overhanging tree branches and speculated on what might happen if their infantry support did not arrive soon. Porter was sure that Sherman would join him presently, and he reassured his command with a bit of levity by stating that, "there was only one road, so he couldn't have taken the wrong one."

RAISE ONE OR THE OTHER

The siege of Charleston harbor was technically raised for a brief time in 1863 by two Confederate ironclads, the *Chicora* and the *Palmetto State*. These two ships had severely damaged several of the Union blockading vessels, and according to maritime law, had caused a hole in the blockade and lifted it. In reality, the hole was plugged up so quickly that there was no opportunity to exploit it, but General P. G. T. Beauregard, standing on the technicality of maritime law, proclaimed that the blockade was lifted and no longer valid to foreign merchantmen. One of the Confederate sailors in Charleston grasped the situation with a little more reality than Beauregard did. "They say we raised the blockade," he wrote, "but we all felt we would have rather raised hell and sank the ships."

EVERY VOTE COUNTS

The Confederate army did succeed in putting the government of the state of Pennsylvania out of the war in 1863 even though it had failed to do so at Gettysburg. The victory was not achieved by force of arms on the battlefield but by sheer luck. Major Henry White, an officer from Pennsylvania, was the reason for this victory. White had run for the state senate while he was serving in the army and had been elected. Before he had the opportunity to serve in his newly elected seat, he was captured in Virginia and sent to Libby Prison in Richmond. The Pennsylvania senate was so evenly split between war and peace factions at that time that all war issues were deadlocked and no votes could be passed for raising troops, appropriating money or accumulating provisions for the active prosecution of the war. White's lone vote would be decisive in breaking the deadlock, and putting Pennsylvania back in the war. The Confederates realized this and made sure that they kept him firmly in their grasp. He was not allowed to correspond with the outside world for fear that he might submit a letter of resignation for his senate seat to proper authorities so that a new election could be held for a candidate who could break the stalemate. So long as White retained his seat, the Confederate government controlled the actions of the Pennsylvania senate. About this time, after the battle at Chickamauga, another Pennsylvanian, Dr. W. S. Hosack was also captured and sent to Libby Prison. He met White, learned of the situation and decided to help. Since Hosack was of no special interest to the Confederates he would undoubtedly be eligible to be exchanged. If he could somehow smuggle White's resignation out of the prison when that day came, he could take it back to Pennsylvania and submit it to the state government for approval. The problem was figuring out a way to get such a document to the North. After much thought, the two arrived at a plan which had obvious merits. Hosack would be able to carry the resignation outright under the Confederate's noses, and they would be none the wiser. White used a piece of toilet paper to write it on and Hosack, taking a button from his coat, removed the stuffing and replaced it with the toilet paper, then sewed the button back in place. When he was exchanged, he went to Indiana, Pennsylvania to the home of Thomas White, the major's father, and presented him with the message from his son. The elder White then hurried the resignation to Governor Andrew G. Curtin. Curtin accepted the document and was thus enabled to declare the seat vacant and hold a special election, in which a candidate of pro-Union sentiments was elected, breaking the deadlock and allowing Pennsylvania to get on with the war.

THE JOKE IS ON US

John Singleton Mosby, then a major, and his command received an assignment from General J. E. B. Stuart in June of 1863 to gather any information available about the intentions of Joe Hooker's Federal forces. Taking three men with him, Mosby assumed a place in the Federal line of march one night. It being dark, the Confederates were not suspected, and were allowed the freedom to ride along the ranks and pick up whatever information they could. As Mosby passed by a house along the road, he noticed a soldier standing in front of the structure holding three horses. The four Confederates asked the orderly who the horses belonged to and were informed that they were owned by two officers who were inside. He further told them that the officers had just come from Hooker's headquarters. These would be just the type of people who could furnish Mosby with the information he wanted, and he lost no time in acting. Calling the orderly over to him, Mosby grabbed the man and whispered, "You are my prisoner.

My name is Mosby." The Federal, an Irishman, did not correctly hear what had just been said to him, and obviously did not take notice of the pistol pointed in his direction. "My name is not Mosby, ye blitherin' idiot," he cried. "I'm as good a Union man as ye are!" "You're the very sort I'm after," Mosby answered, without releasing his grip. At this point, the two officers came out of the house and Mosby engaged them in friendly conversation, while two of his own men approached the officers, hands outstretched to accept their weapons. The Federals mistook this gesture as a handshake and put out their hands in return. At last, they saw the revolvers that were leveled at them and realized what was happening. This realization sent them into a fit of laughter, much to the amazement of Mosby. When asked why they were laughing, the two responded that it had always been a great joke between them when they heard of other soldiers being spirited away by Mosby; now the joke was on them.

Colonel John S. Mosby. The "Gray Ghost" became something of an apparition to Federal outposts during the war, and many Northern soldiers anticipated their turn to be captured by the partisan ranger and his men.

Courtesy of Richard Heiler

IN A RAGE

It is generally assumed that when men fight on the same side in a war that they are able to get along with one another. After all, when you are risking your lives together, fighting for the common cause, it is natural that a bond of association forms. Though this is usually the trend, it need not always be so as shown by an incident which occurred between General Nathan Bedford Forrest and General Braxton Bragg. It seems that Bragg issued an order after the Battle of Chickamauga directing that Forrest transfer the bulk of his command to General Joe Wheeler's Cavalry Corps, retaining but one regiment and one battery for himself. Forrest was enraged by the order, especially since it was not the first time that it had happened. Bragg had issued a similar order during the Kentucky Campaign which had transferred virtually all of Forrest's first command away from him. Some generals might have written to Bragg or started a petition to reverse the order but that would not have been consistent with Forrest's personality. Instead, the cavalry commander paid Bragg a visit in person. He stormed into the commanding general's headquarters, ignoring the salute of the sentry posted outside, and, refusing to shake the commander's outstretched hand, opened with a tirade. "You robbed me of my command in Kentucky, men whom I armed and Equiped [*sic*]...You drove me into West Tennessee in the Winter of 1862, with a second brigade I had organized, with improper arms and without sufficient ammunition...In spite of all this I returned well equiped [*sic*] by captures...and now this second brigade, organized and equiped [*sic*] without thanks to you or the government...you have taken from me. I have stood your meaness [*sic*] as long as I intend to." Forrest then went on to call Bragg a "damned scoundrel," and stated that if Bragg "were any part a man" he would slap his jaw and make him resent it. He concluded his outburst by telling Bragg, "You may as well not issue any orders to me, for I will not obey them, and...if you ever again try to interfere with me or cross my path it will be at the peril of your life."

THE DEVIL MADE ME DO IT

When General John Palmer had posted his Union brigade in position at Corinth to receive an attack from Generals Stirling Price and Van Dorn, General John Pope sent an orderly to ask if he thought his men could hold. "Tell General Pope that I can hold my position against the world, the flesh and the devil," was Palmer's spirited reply. When the Confederate blow fell, Palmer could not back up his boast and his brigade was forced to give ground. Later, when he reported to headquarters, he was greeted with a round of hearty laughter. "How is it, Palmer?" asked Pope. "Well, General, I can stand the world, but the devil was too much for me," said Palmer.

A CLOSE CALL

General John Hunt Morgan's raid through Ohio almost cost that officer his life when he entered the town of Senecaville. Descriptions of Morgan, along with occasional pictures, had been run in the newspapers, and as he rode through the town with his command he was quickly recognized by the inhabitants. Morgan stopped to ask directions at the home of the village milliner. As he strode up the walk, he did not realize the impending danger that was facing him. The woman, wife of an Ohio volunteer, had been given a revolver by her husband for protection, and upon seeing Morgan she fetched it from the drawer where it was kept. Just as the general raised his hand to knock on the door, she aimed the revolver through the parlor window and prepared to squeeze the trigger. But alas, she could not. "What anguish I would cause some woman of the South!" she thought. The revolver was placed back in the drawer and she answered the door. Morgan apologized for the intrusion and asked if she could tell him the best route to Campbell's Station. His question was answered, and the pair talked for a few minutes before Morgan turned to leave. For some reason that she could not explain, the woman called Morgan back and told him what she had almost done and how close he had come to death. Morgan was moved by her words. "Do you know why you did not shoot?" he asked. "At that very moment, Mrs. Morgan, at our home in Tennessee, was down on her knees praying for my safety. I know she was, because a year ago when I was in great danger and as near death as I just was here, I learned on my return home that Mrs. Morgan was on her knees praying for me at that very moment."

HAIL, CAESAR

Headquarters for the Army of the Potomac was an elaborate and formal place. The commanders of this army had become accustomed to a great deal of pomp and circumstance. There were large numbers of tents belonging to the aides and other members of the commanding general's staff, an honor guard dressed in showy Zouave uniforms, and a large headquarters flag bearing a golden eagle in a silver wreath on a solfernio background. The scene presented such a grand picture that the first time Ulysses S. Grant saw it he was led to inquire if Imperial Caesar lived anywhere nearby.

POWERFUL PERSUASION

General John B. Gordon was an inspiration to his men when the time for fighting drew near. He could arouse in them an emotional sense of duty through his pre-battle speeches, and his battlefield examples served to steel the weakest nerve among them. One soldier of his command did not like the general's inspirational presence. He stated that he always hated to hear him speak before a battle, and a comrade asked him to explain. "Because he makes me feel like I could storm hell," the soldier said.

LEE AND THE YANKEE

A Union veteran told a story of how he came to realize that goodness and honor did not reside only in the camps of the Northern armies. It seems that this man had been a bitter anti-Southern advocate, and had taken every opportunity to denounce the Confederates and their cause. On the third day of fighting at Gettysburg, he was badly wounded by a ball which shattered his left leg. As the wounded soldier lay there on the ground, who should ride by but General Lee and his staff. The soldier recognized the Confederate chief, and raising himself up as much as he could, shouted in as defiant a voice as he could muster, "Hurrah for the Union!" Lee heard his taunt, reigned in Traveller, dismounted and began to walk towards him. The poor soldier's first thought was that he was about to be killed because of his remark, but looking up into Lee's face, he lost all apprehension of harm. Lee bore a sad, sympathetic countenance, and he extended his hand in friendship saying, "My son, I hope you will soon be well." The revelation that an enemy could be compassionate towards a fallen foe shook the soldier's beliefs to their foundation. "If I live a thousand years I shall never forget the expression on General Lee's face," he said. "There he was, defeated, retiring from a field that had cost him and his cause almost their last hope, and yet he stopped to say words like those to a wounded soldier of the opposition who had taunted him as he passed by! As soon as the General had left me I cried myself to sleep there upon the bloody ground."

YOU CAN'T BELIEVE HIM

General Nathan Bedford Forrest was once surrounded by a group of Federal soldiers who demanded his immediate surrender. Trapped, the general had to employ brain power to get himself out of the jam. He told his would be captors that he had already surrendered and that he was in the process of going to get the rest of his command so that it could be surrendered when they had stopped him. The Federals, taken in by the story, allowed Forrest to go back to his command unmolested, and once there, he continued to fight with never a thought to surrender.

OLD ACQUAINTANCES

General Daniel Sickles took matters into his own hands when he moved his III Corps line forward from its assigned position on Cemetery Ridge, on the second day of fighting at Gettysburg. Even though he was acting contrary to orders, Sickles took responsibility for the action, trusting his own judgment above that of his superiors. Sickles had always been a strong-willed man when it came to backing up his own convictions, and he felt himself in the right. Before the war, he had shot and killed Phillip Barton Key, the son of Francis Scott Key, author of "The Star-Spangled Banner," because he felt that Key was toying with the affections and honor of his wife. In the subsequent trial, Sickles was acquitted of the charge of murder with the help of a learned lawyer who handled his defense. Sickles would have an opportunity to work with this lawyer in a military capacity during the war as his lawyer had been Edwin Stanton, Lincoln's future secretary of war.

A MOTHER'S LOVE

A woman, of advanced years, went to the White House to make a request of President Lincoln. Waiting her turn, she was ushered into his presence. She told Lincoln that her husband and her three sons had all joined the army and that her husband had recently been killed. Would it now be possible for her oldest son to be released from the service? "Certainly," said Lincoln, "if your prop is taken away, you are justly entitled to one of your boys." He then wrote out an order for the discharge of her son. When the woman reached the army, she found that her eldest son had been wounded and sent to the hospital. The wound proved mortal, however, and by the time she reached the hospital her son was dead. The surgeon in charge wrote the details of what had happened on the back of the president's order and the brokenhearted woman went back to Washington to see Lincoln once more. The president was touched by the incident and said to her, "I know what you wish me to do now, and I shall do it without your asking. I shall release to you your second son." At that, he immediately took up his pen and began to write the order. All the while, the woman was standing beside him, tears running down her cheeks, stroking his hair with a tender, motherly touch. By the time he had finished penning the order, the president's eyes were moist and as he handed her the paper he said, "Now, you have one and I have one of the other two left; that is no more than right." Taking the paper, she once more placed her hand upon his head and said, "The Lord bless you, Mr. President! May you live a thousand years, and always be the head of this great nation!"

THROWN OUT OF COURT

Admiral David D. Porter was an old salt who believed that the purpose of the navy was to join with the enemy and defeat him in open combat. In the operations around Vicksburg, Mississippi, his ships performed invaluable service to Grant's forces in bringing about the surrender of the city. Once during the campaign, one of Porter's ships was sunk by a mine in the Yazoo River. The ship's captain, Thomas Selfridge, reported such to Porter, and seeing that he was agitated by the news said, "I suppose you will want to hold a court." "Courts! I have no time to order courts!" Porter raged. "I can't blame any officer who seeks to put his ship close to the enemy. Is there any other vessel you would like to have?" That was the end of it. Porter did not like losing a ship, but he would not punish an officer who had done so in the act of taking bold measures.

YOU PICK IT

During the fighting at Chickamauga, Colonel John Croxton was ordered by General George Thomas to take his brigade and attack an isolated Confederate brigade that was supposed to be in his front. Croxton promptly obeyed, but soon discovered that what was supposed to be a single brigade was, in fact, Forrest's cavalry and Walker's Corps. Croxton held his desperate position until reinforcements could be sent to him despite the overwhelming disparity of numbers. In the middle of this unequal struggle, he sent a message back to Thomas which showed that being in a tight situation had not caused him to lose his sense of humor. The message asked Thomas to clarify exactly which of the four or five enemy brigades in front of him was the one he was supposed to capture.

THE SPIRIT OF AMERICA

A story was circulated after the Battle of Gettysburg that an apparition in the form of George Washington, mounted upon a white charger, had been seen by many of the men on the battlefield. Once, long after the war, someone asked Joshua Chamberlain if he had heard of the story and if he believed there was any truth in it. Chamberlain took a long time before replying, then said: "Yes, that report was circulated through our lines and I have no doubt that it had a tremendous psychological effect in inspiring the men. Doubtless it was a superstition, but yet who among us can say that such a thing is impossible? We have not yet sounded or explored the immortal life that lies out beyond the Bar [sic]. We know not what mystic power may be possessed by those who now bivouac with the dead. I only know the effect, but I dare not explain or deny the cause. I do believe that we were enveloped by powers of the other world that day and who shall say that Washington was not among the number of those who aided the country that he founded?"

A CHRISTIAN KNIGHT

General Stephen Ramseur was a devoutly religious man. High minded in his ideals, he conducted himself according to the strict code of the Southern Christian gentleman. A story is told of him concerning an incident at Gettysburg where he forgot himself for a moment in the heat of battle which accurately describes the character of the man. Ramseur's brigade was engaged with the Federals and Ramseur had requested artillery support. Repeatedly, he sent the request until finally he turned to a courier and shouted, "Damn it, tell them to send a battery! I have sent for one a dozen times." The words were barely out of his mouth before he threw up both arms and looking skyward said, "God Almighty, forgive me that oath!"

FINDING THE RIGHT PLACE

During one stage of the Battle of Champion Hill favored the Confederates and it appeared that the entire battle might go their way if something was not done by the Federals to stop it. Union officers did stop the Confederate onslaught by steadying their men and stiffening resistance to the point that it broke the Confederate assault and won the day for the North. General John Logan was instrumental in effecting this change in fortunes, and as one enlisted man of the 34th Indiana, J. B. Harris, told of Logan: "After losing one-third of the regiment in killed and wounded and being out of ammunition, [we] were ordered to fall back... While on the retreat we came across General Logan, who shouted...'What regiment is that?'" "...Hearing that it was the 34th Indiana, he said that Indiana should not be disgraced, and we must stop right there. Of course we stopped, and as our adjutant came riding up the general said, 'Adjutant, get your men together.'" "General, the rebels are awful thick up there," said the adjutant. "Damn it! That's the place to kill them—where they are thick!" shouted Logan.

EXPLOSIVE PERSONALITY

During a raid against the Nashville and Decatur Railroad, General Nathan Bedford Forrest happened to come upon a captured caisson stuck in the mud. Though the crew was making all efforts to extricate it, the caisson would not budge. Forrest rode up to the spot and demanded, "Who has charge here?" "I have, sir," replied Captain Andrew McGregor. "Then why in hell don't you do something?" Forrest yelled, followed by a stream of profane expletives. "I'll not be cursed out by anyone, even a superior officer," said McGregor as he grabbed a lighted torch and shoved it into the ammunition chest in an apparently suicidal gesture. Forrest put spurs to his horse and rode away from the caisson as fast as he could, not stopping until he had reached what he felt was a safe distance. He then asked his staff, "What infernal lunatic is that just out of the asylum down there? He came near to blowing himself and me up with a whole caisson full of powder." The staff broke into uncontrollable laughter at the general's inquiry, for they had been aware that the powder had been removed from the caisson some time before. Forrest joined in the laughter once the situation was explained to him, but it was observed thereafter that he never again cursed McGregor.

IN THE DOG HOUSE

General Samuel Beatty's brigade saw its share of fighting in the Civil War, but it will be known to history for something other than a gallant charge or a hard-pressed stand against overwhelming odds. The brigade was issued shelter tents which the men soon discovered were not tall enough to stand up in. In fact, the men claim they were hardly bigger than the space which would be required to shelter a dog. Signs were hung on the fronts of many tents which read: "Pups for sale," or "Terriers," or "Sons of bitches within." When General William Rosecrans visited the brigade camp on an inspection, he was greeted by soldiers who got down on their hands and knees yelling, "Bow wow!" Rosecrans found the sight quite amusing and he promised to try to find better living quarters for the men. The small tents had found a name that stuck though, and always thereafter they would be known to the army as "pup tents."

A HIGH PRIVATE

A Federal soldier, private Henry Castle, was ordered by his colonel to go and find the location of the divisional quartermaster and requisition a daily ration of beef for the regiment from him. Private Castle found a row of white tents belonging to the headquarters of the division, but there was only one man to be seen anywhere around them. The private inquired as to the location of the quartermaster's tent, and as he did so, his horse almost ran into the stranger. As the stranger stepped back, he asked, "Who the hell are you, anyhow?" "Oh, I'm a high private of respectable parentage, like yourself," Castle responded. The stranger laughed at the joke. "What do you want?" he asked. "The quartermaster." "Yes," said the stranger, "but what do you want of him?" Castle was about to tell the man it was none of his business, but reconsidering, gave a brief explanation of his mission. The man spewed forth at once with detailed instructions about what Castle should do. His interest in and knowledge about the completion of the private's mission caused that man to regard him with respect. Just as he was finishing his instructions, a staff officer approached, and holding out a piece of paper said, "General Sheridan, I want your instructions on this matter." Sheridan turned to the private with a smile, explaining that he was never too busy to help with any information he possessed. As Private Castle stated, Sheridan's subsequent success and advancement was a surprise to everyone except the men who had served under him. Here was a man who understood the importance of details.

MAY I CUT IN?

General John Hunt Morgan carried out his missions against the Federal forces he faced as if he knew what their plans and orders were in advance of his actions. In fact, this was more often than not the case. Morgan had a telegraph operator in his unit, and he made a habit of tapping into the telegraph line and having his operator listen in on the Federals. One of Morgan's most important objectives on any campaign was the Federal railroad telegraph offices along his route. He would charge and capture the office, before an alarm could be sounded, and then would substitute his own man for the operator who had been on duty at the time, garnering a wealth of information about his opponent's intentions in the process. This was no small accomplishment when one considers that, among veteran telegraph operators, a man's style of sending a message was as distinctive as his signature. Morgan's man was usually able to copy the operator's style so well that he could communicate with Union operators on the line for hours without them becoming suspicious that any switch had been made.

WHERE ARE THE REINFORCEMENTS?

When Longstreet's crushing attack fell upon the III Corps on the second day of fighting at Gettysburg, it looked as if the Confederates would carry the day. General George Meade shifted men from his other positions to meet the threat, but for a time, the decision hung in the balance and victory could have gone to either side. A particular gap in the Union line worried Meade, and though he had sent for men from another sector to plug it up, they were not yet on the scene. Meade could see the standards of a Confederate regiment advancing towards the gap, and he chose a bold course of action. Along with four members of his immediate staff, he plugged the gap, with full intentions of holding it for as long as the little group could. The four aides were dumbstruck by his action, but they followed his example. When he straightened himself in his saddle, the other men did the same. When the general drew his sabre, four more echoed the rattle. The little band was prepared to stand firmly by their commander and his decision, but they could not help straining their eyes in the direction from which the expected reinforcements were to come. On came the Confederates, and just when it seemed that their fate was sealed, the rattle of infantry on the move in their rear signaled the arrival of the Union troops Meade had requested. With a sigh of relief, the aides returned their swords to their scabbards and looked on as the troops formed into line of battle and engaged the Confederates. Meade's handling of the army at Gettysburg proved to all that he possessed the necessary talent to control an army in battle. His resolve to make a stand at the gap in the lines proved that he also had the personal resolve and bravery to accept any challenge.

HOLDING THE HILL

General George G. Meade was ordered to reconnoiter one of the roads south of the Rappahannock in the opening days of the Chancellorsville Campaign. He pushed his troops forward, and after examining the ground came to the decision that it could be taken and held. At that moment, orders arrived from General Hooker for Meade to report at once to his headquarters. While there, he learned that General George Sykes had taken some high ground in his front, but was being pressured by superior forces under Stonewall Jackson. Sykes thought he could hold on until reinforcements arrived, and Meade, having surveyed the ground, believed him. He was dismayed, therefore, to learn that Hooker was ordering Sykes to fall back from his strong position. Turning to some officers near him, he said in disgust, "My God, if we can't hold the top of a hill, we certainly can't hold the bottom of it!"

Major General George G. Meade and staff. Many of these officers during the battle were anxiously looking for Federal reinforcements when Meade decided to hold a part of the Union line at Gettysburg personally. This photograph is subsequent to the Battle of Gettysburg.

THE GRIM, FINAL YEARS

TEMPERS RISE

On April 2, 1863 the city of Richmond was invaded not from without, but from within. On that day, five hundred women and boys gathered in Capitol Square to protest the lack of food which the inhabitants of the city had been experiencing. Their protest soon turned into a riot as the mob vandalized store fronts and took what they wanted from the shops of unlucky merchants. President Jefferson Davis happened on the scene before the local Home Guard could arrive to restore order, and he tried to reason with the crowd. Climbing to the bed of a wagon, he pleaded with his audience to give up this action and peaceably return to their homes. His request was met with jeers and accusations from the mob. One member of the crowd threw a loaf of bread at him. The president caught the loaf, and waiving it in the air chided, "Bread is so plentiful that you throw it away!"

Confederate President Jefferson Davis. After the Battle of Chickamauga, Davis promoted a junior brigadier in the Army of Tennessee because his trail of dead horses on the battlefield showed marked courage.

Leib Image Archives

DON'T MAKE ME CRY

One day the wife of one of John Singleton Mosby's men came to the White House to see President Lincoln. Her husband had been captured and was sentenced to be shot, and she came to beg the president for mercy. Lincoln listened as she told her story and then asked her what kind of husband he was.

"Is he intemperate, does he abuse the children and beat you?"

"No, no," the wife replied. "He is a good man, a good husband; he loves me and he loves the children and we cannot live without him. The only trouble is that he is a fool about politics. I live in the North and was born there, and if I get him home he will do no more fighting for the South."

Lincoln examined the papers and said, "Well, I will pardon him and turn him over to you for safekeeping."

At this, the woman's relief was so great that she began to sob uncontrollably.

"My dear woman," Lincoln said, "if I had known how badly it was going to make you feel, I never would have pardoned him."

"You do not understand Me [*sic*]," the woman sobbed.

"Yes, yes, I do," replied Lincoln, "and if you do not go away at once I shall be crying with you."

NO PEEPING TOMS

The Union and Confederate soldiers in one sector of the Petersburg trenches had made an informal truce among themselves and they enjoyed a respite from the fighting which was taking place along the rest of the line. The only time it was not safe for a soldier on either side to raise his head above the trench was when an officer showed up. Officers were viewed as interlopers by both sides in this quiet sector, and all that the troops who were facing each other wished for was to be left alone. A Union officer, General Samuel Crawford, came to examine the line at this point and with binoculars in hand, climbed to the top of the earthworks and began to scan the Rebel position. No sooner had he done so than a rock with a message around it was tossed into the Union trenches. One of the soldiers picked up the rock and read the contents of the note to Crawford. "Tell the fellow with the spy glass to clear out or we shall have to shoot him."

CLAIM TO FAME

The election of 1864 went to Lincoln and the Republican party by a narrow margin of popular vote, even though the electoral vote was heavily in Lincoln's favor. Had it not been for the soldier vote which was made possible through mass furloughs, the Democrats would have, in all probability, succeeded in gathering the majority of popular votes in enough states to have unseated Lincoln and brought the war to a close under a negotiated peace.

Alleged fear of rioting in New York City led Ben Butler, military commander of the Department of Virginia and North Carolina, to place observers at the polling stations and to hold four regiments of troops in readiness on ferry boats, ready to "land and march double quick across the island," in case of Democratic disturbances. After the war, when Butler was reviewing his military career, he denied that any fame should come his way due to the Louisiana Campaign. "I do not claim to be the hero of New Orleans," he said. "Farragut has that high honor; but I do claim to be the hero of New York City in the election of 1864, when they had an honest election, the only one before or since."

TO TELL THE TRUTH

Joseph E. Johnston was loved by his men in the Army of Tennessee; so much so that many of his troops did not believe it when they heard that he had been replaced by John Bell Hood in command of that army. One story tells of how a soldier in the Confederate ranks learned the news of the change in command.

A Federal picket yelled, "Johnny, O, Johnny, O, Johnny Reb [sic]."

"What do you want?" yelled his Confederate counterpart.

"Joe Johnston is relieved of command," shouted the Yank.

"What?! [sic]"

"General Joseph E. Johnston is relieved, and Hood appointed in his place," the Yank explained.

"You're a damned liar!" shouted the Reb. "Come out and show yourself and I'll shoot you in your tracks."

After some bitter exchanges the two men stepped out into the open and began firing at one another. They kept up their duel until the Confederate fell to the ground with a bullet in his heart. Joe Johnston was his commander until the time he died.

AN ACT OF CHARITY

Christmas of 1864 found Robert E. Lee's Army of Northern Virginia short on almost everything but grit and determination. The Confederacy had been reduced by Sherman's march, to a few disconnected segments, united in name and spirit only. The South had lost the ability to support its armies, and the nation could endure only as long as its troops could suffer the hardships of want. Lee ate the slightest of holiday dinners that Christmas, foregoing the traditional turkey feast. A turkey had been provided; several, in fact, had been sent to Lee and his staff by grateful citizens just before the holiday, but the commanding general could not think of enjoying them himself while his men did without. "I don't know what you are going to do with your turkeys," he told his staff, "but I wish mine sent to the hospital in Petersburg." The staff followed his example and the wounded in Petersburg were treated to turkey for Christmas.

TALK SENSE

As William T. Sherman and John Bell Hood maneuvered for position after the evacuation of Atlanta the motives of the Confederate commander were shrouded in mystery. Every time Sherman would calculate the meaning of Hood's most recent move, he would do something that was exactly the opposite of that which was expected. Sherman complained of this fact to a subordinate officer once saying: "I can not guess his movements as I could those of Johnston who was a sensible man and only did sensible things."

DON'T TAKE ME WITH YOU

During the Georgia Campaign, shortly before his death, General Leonidas Polk requested an officer to accompany him to a ridge which gave a superior view of the Federal position. Union gunners soon spotted the two officers silhouetted upon the height, and shells began to fall around them. The concussion of the bombs stunned both men and threw them to the ground. Several minutes time passed as they lay there, but finally, Polk's companion recovered, and cast a glassy look around to see what had become of the general. Polk lay close by, and his companion could see that he was starting to come around. A few moments later the general muttered, "Oh, Lord! where am I, where am I?"

The companion was not noted for his piety or reverence as Polk was, the bishop-general of the army, and he saw a chance to have some fun with his friend. Leaning over to Polk, he whispered gently, "In Hell, General."

"Impossible," muttered the still half-conscious general. "Who is it that tells me so?"

His companion leaned over once more to reveal his identity, which caused Polk to groan and state that if he was there, then indeed he must be in hell!

SEND THEM HOME

Robert E. Lee fought against the North out of a sense of duty to his home state of Virginia, not because of any hatred or resentment for the government or the people of the North. A master in the art of war, he, nonetheless, detested the bloodshed which this war had caused. After the Battle of Spotsylvania, General Jubal Early voiced a sentiment which could have found strong support among many Confederates. "I wish they were all dead," he said in referring to the Federal army. Lee did not agree. "I wish they were all at home," he replied, "attending to their own business, leaving us to do the same."

FINDING A FORD

During the Confederate siege of the Union forces bottled up in the city of Chattanooga, it was a common occurrence for the pickets of both armies to engage in conversations and swapping of material goods. At one point along the lines, the pickets were separated by the Tennessee River, which was several hundred yards wide, but this did not stop their friendly interchange. Instead, they would swim to a small island midway across the river, and then exchange news of the war, papers, tobacco, and coffee. Colonel John Wilder, commander of Federal mounted infantry at Chattanooga, was well aware of the informal truces, and he decided to make an asset out of them. Approaching the river's bank, he called across to the Confederates on the opposite shore, and a meeting was set up at the island as usual. The Confederate picket jumped into the river and swam to his destination, but Wilder waded the distance, explaining to the Reb that he could not swim. Since he wore no insignia of rank, the Confederate did not suspect that this was anything more than another informal truce, and he invited the Yankee to come across to the Southern lines with him. Wilder accepted, and as his host swam back to his side of the river he waded behind. Once his visit among the Confederates was over, Wilder stepped back into the water and waded back to the Union lines, and as far as the Southerners were concerned that was the end of it. Not so, for the reason Wilder had refused to swim the river was that he was searching for a ford that he could use to cross his troops when the Union army attacked to lift the siege.

A FOREIGN IMPORT

Due to the cramped and unsanitary conditions in which surgeons of both armies were forced to work, most wounds occurring in limbs were routinely treated by means of amputation. So routine did this procedure become that many soldiers declared that their arms and legs had been amputated for a simple flesh wound. Supplications from the unfortunate patients to save their limbs almost always went for naught and they awoke from anesthetic to find a bandaged stump where their arm or leg had been.

At Peach Tree Creek, Thomas Reynolds, an Irishman by birth, was shot in the leg and taken to the hospital for treatment. As the doctors discussed the reasons why the leg had to be amputated, Reynolds tried in vain to change their minds. Finally, he stated that the leg must be saved as it was an imported one and therefore more valuable than those of the ordinary variety. This piece of wit so disarmed the doctors that they bowed to his wishes and saved the leg.

LET ME DO MY JOB

General Henry Wise once drove an interloping civilian out of camp with a bombardment of profane oaths. When the civilian got back to Richmond, he spread the tale of how rudely he had been treated by Wise and eventually the story found its way back to Robert E. Lee. A few days later, Lee visited Wise, and in the course of the evening suggested that they take a walk together.

"I suspected what was coming," stated Wise. "After telling me of the complaints made of my treatment of the Richmond man, and hearing my account of the affair, not omitting the apology and broadside, he laid his hand upon my arm, and with that grace and cordiality, which, at times, tempered his usual stately dignity, said, 'Wise, you know as well as I do what the army regulations say about profanity. But, as an old friend, let me ask you if that dreadful habit cannot be broken—and remind you that we have both already passed the meridian of life, etc.' Seeing he was in for a sermon, and one that I could not answer, I replied, 'General Lee, you certainly play Washington to perfection, and your whole life is a constant reproach to me. Now, I am perfectly willing that Jackson and yourself shall do the praying for the whole Army of Northern Virginia, but, in Heaven's name, let me do the cussin' for one small brigade.' Lee laughed and said, 'Wise, you are incorrigible.'" The two officers then walked to Wise's quarters and the subject was pursued no further.

CHANGE OF HEART

Abraham Lincoln did not enjoy the same fame while he was living that his memory commands now. In fact, he was constantly the object of schemes to either diminish his power or set him out of office altogether. Horace Greeley, owner of the powerful *New York Tribune*, backed one plan to oust the president and replace him with someone more to his own liking. His choice for a successor to Lincoln was General William S. Rosecrans, and he sent one of his employees, James R. Gilmore, to Murfreesboro to talk to the general, evaluate his possibilities as a potential candidate and feel him out as to the likelihood of running for high office.

Gilmore's interview with Rosecrans was a flop. The general had no intentions of seeking political office for himself, and he held all polititians in contempt. Gilmore had opportunity to interview Lincoln a short time after meeting with Rosecrans and was so taken with the president's logic and common sense that he changed his political affiliations and became one of Lincoln's strongest supporters for a second term.

A SMALL PACKAGE

Alexander Stephens, the vice president of the Confederacy, was not a large man in size. In fact, he was rather on the small side, possibly weighing under one hundred pounds. When he met with President Lincoln and Secretary William Seward as a member of the Peace Commission at Hampton Roads he wore a full overcoat which made him appear as a man who was much larger. Only when he removed his coat could his true size be seen. After the meeting was over, Lincoln commented to Seward: "I say Seward, did you notice that coat Alec Stephens wore?" Seward answered in the affirmative. "Never have I seen so small a nubbin come out of so much husk," Lincoln said.

THE UNDEFEATED

General Patrick Cleburne was one of the hardest hitting divisional commanders in the Confederate army. His division of veterans was respected and admired by the Southern troops, respected and feared by the Yankees. General William Hardee paid tribute to the man and his soldiers in words which define the spirit and character of Cleburne's Division as eloquently as is possible. "When Cleburne's division defended, no odds broke its lines; where it attacked, no numbers resisted its onslaught, save only once, and there is the grave of Cleburne."

A GOOD JUDGE OF CHARACTER

During Joe Johnston's retrograde movement towards Atlanta in the summer of 1864, the general came under a great deal of criticism from his antagonists in the military and in the government. His friends maintained that the movement was strategic and that Johnston would not only stand and fight, but would defeat the Federal army which Sherman was leading, when the time for action was right. Southern newspapers picked up on the theme of Johnston's supporters, that the general had things well in hand, and they even ran a quotation of General Winfield Scott's that had been made earlier in the war. Scott had warned to "beware of Lee advancing, and watch Johnston at a stand; for the devil would be defeated in the attempt to whip him retreating."

ETERNAL REST

On a march from Florence, Alabama to Columbia, Tennessee, General Patrick Cleburne happened to pass by St. John's Episcopal Church, a vine-covered, gothic structure which was so beautiful and peaceful it led the general to comment that it was almost worth dieing "to be buried in such a beautiful spot." The march continued and resulted in the battles of Spring Hill and Franklin. In the latter, General Cleburne was killed while leading a charge against the Union lines. His remains were interred at St. John's, the cemetery he said was beautiful enough to die for.

VALIANT IN VICTORY

Throughout the ages, it has been the custom of a victorious general to lead his army into a captured city. Ulysses S. Grant had the opportunity to do so when the city of Richmond fell, and no one would have denied him the right to enter the Confederate capital in triumph. When news of Richmond's evacuation reached Grant's headquarters, his wife inquired as to his intentions for traveling to the city. "I would not distress these people," he said. "They are feeling their defeat bitterly, and you would not add to it by my witnessing their despair, would you?"

PRESIDENTIAL PREMONITIONS

Abraham Lincoln had several premonitions involving his own death, the best known of which is his dream of being on a ship heading towards a dark, indefinite shore. Though the allusion here can definitely be linked to his death, the dream is still interpretive in its meaning. The president did have a more graphic dream on the subject during the last days of his life. He had walked into the East Room of the White House and had seen a coffin laying there. When he asked who it was that was inside the coffin, the person in his dream answered, "The President."

BAD LUCK

General Braxton Bragg endured a disappointing tenure as the commander of the Confederate Army of Tennessee. While his army performed well in every engagement, it was defeated by the Federals almost every time out. The Army of Tennessee's luck against the Federals became so bad that a joke was popular among its ranks that Bragg could "snatch defeat from the jaws of victory."

MAN OF HIS WORD

George Meade and Phil Sheridan had a run-in on May 8, 1864 which had far-reaching effects on the combat efficiency of the Army of the Potomac. Sheridan and his cavalry were to clear the Confederates from a certain stretch of road and they had failed to do so. Some of the fault lay with Sheridan, but Meade was also to blame for he had changed some of Sheridan's orders without telling him.

Later, when Sheridan came to army headquarters, Meade greeted him with angry denunciations for letting his cavalry get in the infantry's way. Sheridan countered that it was all Meade's fault for countermanding his orders and that he could go out and whip J. E. B. Stuart's force at any time if he would just be allowed to use the cavalry as it should be used.

Up to this time, the Union cavalry had too often been used as a staff outfit, detailed to guarding trains, scouting, and serving as couriers. The first time the cavalry corps was brought together was when Joe Hooker had commanded the army. What Sheridan was angry about was more the way the cavalry was being used than what had happened that day. He wanted to use it as a strong striking force, much the same as Stuart used his cavalry.

When Meade went to see Grant and tell him about what had transpired, Grant saw through to the root of the problem at once. As Meade related how Sheridan had boasted that he could whip Stuart if he was allowed to take the cavalry out on his own, Grant looked up.

"Did Sheridan say that?" he asked. "Well, he generally knows what he is talking about. Let him start right out and do it."

Major General Philip H. Sheridan. A stickler for detail, Sheridan's organizational skills and personal attention to the little things made him a natural leader of men and a dangerous adversary of the battlefield.

Courtesy of Richard Heiler

GAME TO THE END

General John Sedgwick was a great tease, and his familiar manner with his men caused him to attain the nickname of "Uncle John." This is not to say that his men viewed him as an easy task master. On the contrary, Sedgwick was one of the most experienced field commanders in the Northern army, and his skill in military matters had won him the respect of the entire Army of the Potomac. The fact that he was a jokester only served to humanize him to the men and make them see him as a regular fellow. During the Battle of Spotsylvania, the general had been exposing himself in a fashion which caused his staff to become alarmed, and one of his aides pointed out that his place was not supposed to be this far in the van of the army. Sedgwick, in classic form, turned to the staff officer and playfully remarked, "McMahon, I would like to know who commands this corps, you or I?" A few minutes later a sharpshooter's bullet found its mark and the general was dead. The army had lost a corps commander and the North had lost a homespun hero.

Major General John Sedgwick. The fun-loving commander of the Union VI Corps. He would go to his death with a good-natured jibe still fresh on his lips.

Courtesy of Richard Heiler

WASTING AMMUNITION

During a pause in the fighting in the Atlanta Campaign, General Mortimer Leggett was puzzled by the silence of the pickets along his front. He sent one of his escorts to find out what was going on and when the man returned, he informed the general that the pickets were "having a chat with the Johnnies." According to the escort, "It made the General mad. He said he didn't put us up there to talk but to shoot, and ordered every man to be given one hundred rounds, and if they didn't use them up, they were to be put on extra duty. It was impossible to shoot them away, so they threw them away. But it almost broke up the fun...."

A GALLANT SHOW

One drawback in commanding volunteer troops is that they have to be led into battle by their commanders at times. Mere orders will not suffice, leadership in its highest form must be used. This explains the high casualty rate suffered by officers during the war and it also explains how so many of them became heroes. General Joshua Chamberlain was leading a charge on March 29, 1865 when he was struck and severely wounded by a bullet. The bullet had hit the general's horse in the neck, then ran up Chamberlain's arm and struck a mirror in his breast pocket, just below his heart, with staggering force. The projectile then traveled around two ribs, eventually exiting through the back seam of the general's coat. Knocked unconscious by the blow, Chamberlain had instinctively wrapped his arms around his horse's neck and had remained in the saddle. When he came to, he was greeted by General Charles Griffin who supposed his friend's wound to be mortal and exclaimed, "My dear General, you are gone."

Chamberlain misunderstood the meaning of Griffin's remark, thinking he had alluded to the fact that Chamberlain was no longer leading the charge. The attack had bogged down on the right and some of the Union troops were making for the rear. Chamberlain lost no time in getting back into the action. He spurred his horse forward to meet the men who were retreating and the sight of the blood-spattered general duly impressed the soldiers who rallied and surged forward again. As Chamberlain rode back towards the center of his line, he was greeted by an uproar of cheering. It was only natural for his own men to be cheering him, but some of the cheers came from a most unexpected quarter; the Confederates in the line his men were assaulting had seen his act and added their voices to those of their enemy in exulting a courageous act.

DON'T LEAVE HOME WITHOUT IT

Ulysses S. Grant was riding on a train, devoid of any insignia of rank, when a boy came through the car crying, "Life of General Grant." In his hand was a copy of a book detailing the general's life which he was selling. "That man might like a copy," said one of Grant's aides, pointing to the general. The boy handed him the book and Grant casually leafed through the pages. "Who is this all about?" he asked when his perusal was complete. The boy gave him a look of utter disgust and replied, "You must be a darned greeny not to know General Grant!" The general did not pursue the matter any further. He bought a copy of his biography, sending the youthful peddler on his way, entirely oblivious to the fact that he had just been in the presence of the great men whose life story he was trying to sell.

THE NAME'S THE SAME

John Singleton Mosby owed a certain measure of his success as a partisan ranger to the fact that he enjoyed the absolute support of the citizens in his theater of operations. A Federal officer in the last months of the war had the opportunity to see for himself just how devoted the people were. This cavalryman had been riding along the west slope of the Blue Ridge when he came upon a cabin. Being thirsty, he decided to ask for a drink of water, but he thought that he had best find out if there were any Confederates nearby. A woman was sitting outside of the cabin and he asked her: "Do you live here alone?"

"Yes," she answered. "Just me and Colonel Mosby."

At that, the officer wheeled his horse around and sped away. Several hours later he returned at the head of a heavily armed detachment of cavalry and demanded, "Get me Colonel Mosby!"

The woman obeyed and went inside the house. When she reappeared outside she was holding her frightened little two-year-old son by the hand, informing the Federals that this was Colonel Mosby, namesake of the partisan leader. The detachment returned to its camp without their prize prisoner, but the men in the ranks had plenty of fun with the officer who had become so concerned over a two-year-old boy.

STEAMER OF A DIFFERENT SORT

Raphael Semmes is known for his daring exploits at sea and has become legendary as a naval captain, but one of his most interesting adventures occurred while he was confined to dry land. Semmes was forced to scuttle his ships during the evacuation of Richmond to keep them from falling into Federal hands. He and his crew were then to join the army in its evacuation.

After the ships had been destroyed, the Confederate Jacks fell in line and, unaccustomed as they were to the drill, proceeded to march to their appointed rendezvous area. When they arrived in the city, Semmes discovered that the last train had already left the station and it appeared that he and his men were doomed to be captured by the advancing Federals. The station was crowded with civilians who had also missed the last train. They were crowded onto a few remaining cars which lay on the track in the hope that someone would come back for them. Semmes scouted the station and was able to find one small engine still there, but the railroad workers to run it had long since fled the scene. Undaunted by this fact, Semmes determined to operate the train himself. He randomly assigned one of his crew as a fireman and one as an engineer and directed a part of his force to tear down a nearby picket fence for fuel. Before long, sufficient steam was built up in the engine's boiler and the Semmes Railroad was in business. The first priority was to hook the engine to the cars and to empty those same cars of their civilian passengers to make room for his sailors, for as Semmes said, it was more important that armed soldiers were not captured. Once the sailors were aboard, it was observed that there was still enough room to accommodate the refugees, and they were hurriedly boarded as well. Semmes gave the order to pull out, and the little engine toiled forward with its heavy load.

It seemed as if Semmes had been successful once more in eluding the Yankees, but just as the train reached the track outside the station yard the little engine stalled under its burden and could pull no more. Lady luck did not forsake the admiral for he soon found another engine, and repeating the procedure he had followed in the station, he was soon on his way again towards the rear of Lee's army. His fame as a sailor was legendary; he had just proven his resourcefulness as a railroadman, and now was off to try his luck with the foot soldiers.

A SOLDIER'S FRIEND

The evacuation of the city of Petersburg left in Union hands a commodity which the soldiers in the ranks were eager to get their hands on, tobacco. Guards were placed at all public buildings, however, and the troops were denied admittance to the tobacco warehouses. This caused a protest from many of the troops who had gathered around a particular warehouse and felt themselves deserving of the contents therein. As they were standing there, cursing their poor luck and the order which barred them from the coveted weed, an older looking man, dressed in civilian clothes and wearing a slouch hat, was seen some distance off observing the scene. The soldiers assumed that he was the owner of the warehouse and a group of them went to ask him if this was the case.

"Well perhaps I do boys," the stranger answered when asked if he was the owner. "Why do you want to know?"

The men were convinced that he was the owner and they asked if he might permit them to have some of the tobacco. The stranger walked over to the entrance of the warehouse and inquired of the guard: "May I see the officer in command please?" He was answered by a young lieutenant in a caustic manner. "Who are you? Do you own this warehouse?"

The stranger was taken aback by the rudeness of the lieutenant's manner, but he asked the question again, "Will you please call your superior officer?"

"Not for any ——— rebel son of a ——— ," was the officer's only reply.

At this, the man took out a notebook and scribbled out a quick note. He then asked if there was an orderly present with a horse who would volunteer to deliver the message to General Grant. A man stepped forward and was soon on his way. Within a matter of minutes, Grant came galloping up to the warehouse in great haste. Dismounting his horse, he shook hands with the stranger and asked: "Mr. President, how can I serve you?"

The lieutenant turned pale when he realized who he had been talking to and he advanced to Lincoln to apologize, fully expecting to be relieved at once. The president did not dismiss him, opting to scold him instead. "Young man, don't always judge by appearances. And treat your elders with more respect in the future." The soldiers were then given ample tobacco to satisfy them for some time to come.

VICTORY PARTY

Sergeant Theodore Upson was surprised one night when he went to take charge of the guard at General Charles R. Woods' tent. The general told him to dismiss the guard and come inside the tent. Upson was taken aback by the general's actions and he asked why the guard was being dismissed.

"Don't you know Lee has surrendered?" Woods asked. "No man shall stand guard at my quarters tonight. Bring all the guard here." When the guard assembled, they were treated to an alcoholic punch inside the general's tent. Toasts to the Union victory abounded and the revelers soon were joined by a band. The band members furnished entertainment to those present, but gradually they became more a part of the party than entertainment, and the music soured as the bandsman played several different songs at the same time. Officers from other units were attracted to Woods' tent by the sound of the merriment within, and what had started as a small affair was now a large gathering.

According to Sergeant Upson: "...General Woods shook my hand and said he would promote me, that I could consider myself a Lieutenant. After a little more talk from Colonel Johnson he made me a captain, and I might have gone higher if the general had not noticed that the band was not playing. Going out to see about it, he found the members on the ground or anything they could find, several on the big bass drum. Then he realized they were tired, very tired, and he would relieve them. He got the big drum, other officers took the various horns and started on a tour through the camps—every fellow blowing his horn to suit himself and the jolly old general pounding the bass drum for all it was worth."

The festivities continued into the wee hours of the morning, then, slowly it began to break up. Upson did not see General Woods for a couple of days, but on that next meeting he was greeted cordially by name by that officer. It seems, however, that the general had forgotten the promotions he had bestowed during the party for he addressed Upson as a sergeant, and sergeant it would stay for the remainder of Upson's time in the service.

TRIBUTE TO ALL

When the blue and the gray met for the surrender ceremonies at Appomattox Court House, an event occurred which was to go a long way towards binding up the wounds of the nation. General Joshua Chamberlain was given the honor of representing the Union forces in the surrender of the Confederate army, and as he saw the Confederates marching towards the position where his troops stood in formation, he was struck by the thought that these brave men in gray were deserving of a tribute for the valorous service they had rendered in their cause. Though he realized that he would be placing himself in line for abusive criticism from politically embittered people in the North, he resolved to order that a salute of arms be given to the Confederates. As he explained it, "My main reason was one for which I sought no authority nor asked forgiveness. Before us in proud humiliation stood the embodiment of manhood: men whom neither toils and sufferings, nor the fact of death, nor disaster, nor hopelessness could bend from their resolve; standing before us now, thin, worn, and famished, but erect, and with eyes looking level into ours, waking memories that bound us together as no other bond; was not such manhood to be welcomed back into the Union so tested and assured?"

Orders were issued to each regimental commander, and when the head of the Confederate column came even with the first Union brigade in formation, regiment by regiment, the Northern troops raised their muskets to the position of the old "carry"—the marching salute.

General John B. Gordon had been riding at the head of the Confederate column, his head thoughtfully bowed, when he heard the shuffling of the Union firearms and realized its meaning. His mood changed at once and he wheeled his horse toward the first Union brigade and dropping his sword, point to his boot, returned the compliment. Turning towards his own column, he then ordered his troops to pass with the same "carry" position. Thus, these two great armies ended their struggle with mutual respect and admiration for one another, earned through hardships and suffering on many bloodstained battlefields.

FINAL ACT

Near the close of the war, a Confederate soldier was captured within the Federal lines in Mississippi and he was held for execution as a spy. The soldier was not actually doing espionage work, but merely delivering letters to the family of his commander, but he was, nonetheless, found guilty of spying in not one but three separate trials and the sentence of death was due to be carried out. An appeal was made to President Lincoln, "in the interest of peace and consideration," to intercede in the condemned man's behalf, which Lincoln promptly did. He directed that the petitioner go to Secretary Stanton and secure the release of the soldier.

Stanton was unyielding to the man's request, refusing to grant a pardon. This sent the petitioner back to the White House for another interview with Lincoln. The president was dressed in formal attire, preparing to go out for the evening when the matter was brought before him again. He took time to write an official order for the unconditional release and pardon of the prisoner saying, "I think this will have precedence over Stanton!" He then left, keeping his schedule for the evening. The date was April 14, 1865 and Lincoln would not return to the White House. The plans for the evening were to go to Ford's Theater to take in a play. There he would meet with the assassin's bullet which would take his life. His last official act as president had been to spare the life of an innocent Confederate soldier.

STOP THE FIGHTING

With the surrender of Joe Johnston's forces in North Carolina it seemed as if all the fighting in the war had come to an end. The issue had been settled and it was hoped that sectional differences would not be heard of again. The war was hardly over, however, before a new sectional dispute erupted which threatened to curb the joy the North felt at the cessation of hostilities. This dispute was not between North and South, rather it was between East and West. Soldiers from western and eastern armies were brought together in Washington for a victory parade to honor their achievements. As men from the different armies visited back and forth between camps, friction began to appear. The western troops claimed that they had done most of the marching and fighting in the war and that if it had not been for them, Lee would never have been cornered. Easterners countered that if Sherman had faced Lee in the west he would never have gotten to the sea and claimed that they spent the last four years fighting against real soldiers instead of the backwoods bushwackers they claimed the western army had dealt with. Insults soon turned into fist fights between individuals and even entire brigades. Double guards had to be placed at each camp; and many officers had to sleep with their swords and revolvers by their side in readiness to keep their own men from fighting each other. In the end, the parade came off as scheduled and there were no further confrontations. The troops of both armies went home to resume civilian life and there was glory and honor enough for all to share.

THE HEALING TIME

A TREASURED GIFT

Robert E. Lee had served as the symbolic leader of the Southern cause throughout the last year of the war. At its end, he became the symbol of the lost cause; the warrior who had battled gallantly against long odds, almost bringing victory to his cause; and the warrior who had sought a just and honorable peace once further resistance became impractical. In the days immediately following the surrender at Appomattox, crowds gathered regularly outside the Richmond residence of Lee. They were made up of paroled soldiers, passing through the city on their way to points farther south, as well as civilians who had come to catch a glimpse of the famous commander. Lee never greeted the crowds, though, and he kept the front shutters of the house closed as he attempted to elude the limelight and assume the role of civilian. Sometimes, members of the crowd would seek and be granted permission to come in the house. One such visitor was a tall ex-soldier who came to Lee with an offer. "General Lee," he said, "I followed you for four years and done the best I knowed how. Me and my wife live on a little farm away up on the Blue Ridge Mountains. If you will come up thar, we will take care of you the best we know how as long as we live." With tears running down his cheeks, Lee clasped the man's hands in his own. "I don't need a thing," he said. "My friends all over the country have been very kind and have sent me more clothes than I can possibly use, so I want to thank you for coming and give you this new suit." The general handed the man a box, containing a civilian suit which Lee intended as a replacement for the worn homespun uniform the man was then wearing. The gift held too much sentiment for the man to use it, however. "General Lee," he said, "I will carry it back home, put it away and when I die the boys will put it on me."

64

General Robert E. Lee. The most celebrated soldier in the South, Lee shunned any of the amenities his position might have brought his way, choosing to live as his men did. Once, he gave away his holiday dinner because he could not enjoy it while there were soldiers from his army going hungry.

A TERRIBLE ENEMY

General Emory Upton rose through the ranks of field command during the Civil War to attain a position of prominence within the army. In the process, he had fought and struggled over most of the Eastern battlefields, and had never faltered in the face of the death and destruction they held for fighting men. After the war, Upton became a renowned authority on military policy and was assigned to the post of commandant at West Point. Upton died in 1881, at the age of forty-two. The cause of death was a gunshot wound to the head, self-inflicted. He had contracted "an incurable malady of the head and its passages that ultimately became unbearable," and though he had escaped the perils of the battlefield on numerous occasions, he was forced to surrender to an ailment which would give him no peace.

INTERNAL STRIFE

Edwin Stanton had labored throughout the Civil War to ensure victory for the Union cause and his efforts towards that end had taken on an almost superhuman air. Though he was not a social man, or one who was easy to get to know or like, all who knew him had to pay tribute to his sacrifices for the cause and his able handling of the War Department.

After the war, President Andrew Johnson attempted to get rid of Stanton, who he viewed as a radical, and offered the post to General Grant. Grant did not wish to become embroiled in the affair so he turned down the offer. The position was then tendered to General Lorenzo Thomas and was accepted by him. Stanton was notified of his dismissal by Johnson, and Thomas was appointed secretary of war *ad interim*, but there was little for him to do. Stanton refused to vacate his post and barricaded himself in his quarters in the War Department, continuing to perform the duties of the office. In the end, Stanton won as the Tenure of Office Act was invoked in his behalf, and this attempt to dismiss him so enraged the Congress, already estranged from the president, that the House voted to impeach Johnson.

FOES NO MORE

After the war, General John Bell Hood and General George Thomas happened to be staying in the same hotel in New Orleans. Hood learned of Thomas' presence and asked a woman in the hotel if she would arrange for a meeting between the two. The woman went to Thomas' room and asked if he would consent to meet with the man against whom he had fought three of his great battles: Chickamauga, Atlanta and Nashville; Thomas, accepted the invitation by saying, "Certainly, my dear madam."

Thomas heard Hood coming down the hallway on his crutches and threw open the door to greet him with a tender embrace. The two talked for about an hour and when their meeting was over the lady who had arranged it had the opportunity to observe Hood, saying that, "the bravest fighter of all the Confederate forces had a trace of tears in his eyes and voice." Hood was taken with Thomas and his comment to the lady showed he bore no malice towards his old foe. "Thomas is a grand man," he said. "He should have remained with us, where he would have been appreciated and loved."

BIBLIOGRAPHY

Alexander, Edward Porter. *Fighting For The Confederacy*. Chapel Hill: University of North Carolina Press, 1989.

Angle, Paul M. *The Lincoln Reader*. New Brunswick: Rutgers University Press, 1947.

Blackford, Susan Leigh. *Letters From Lee's Army*. New York: A. S. Barnes & Co., 1962.

Brooks, Elbridge S. *The True Story of U. S. Grant*. Boston: Lothrup Publishing Co., 1897.

Cleaves, Freeman. *Meade of Gettysburg*. Dayton: Morningside Bookshop, 1980.

Davis, Burke. *They Called Him Stonewall*. New York: The Fairfax Press, 1988.

Davis, Burke. *To Appomattox: Nine April Days, 1865*. Eastern Acorn Press, 1981.

Davis, William C. *Battle at Bull Run*. Baton Rouge: Louisiana State University Press, 1977.

Foote, Shelby. *The Civil War: A Narrative*. New York: Random House, 1958.

Gibson, John. *Those 163 Days: A Southern Account of Sherman's March From Atlanta to Raleigh*. New York: Brainhall House, 1961.

Glatthaar, Joseph. *The March to the Sea and Beyond: Sherman's Troops in the Savannah and Carolina Campaign*. New York: New York University Press, 1986.

Hansen, Harry. *The Civil War*. New York: Mentor Books, 1961.

Happel, Ralph. *Salem Church Embattled*. Eastern National Park & Monument Association, 1980.

Hassler, Warren W., Jr. *Commanders of the Army of the Potomac*. Baton Rouge: Louisiana State University Press, 1962.

Hertz, Emanuel. *Lincoln Talks*. New York: Brainhall House, 1986.

Hoehling, A. A., and Mary Hoehling. *The Last Days of the Confederacy*. New York: The Fairfax Press, 1981.

Horgan, Paul. *Citizen of New Salem*. New York: Farrar, Straus and Cudahy, 1961.

Jones, J. B. *A Rebel War Clerk's Diary at the Confederate Capital*. Philadelphia: J. B. Lippincott & Co., 1866.

Jones, Virgil Carrington. *Gray Ghosts and Rebel Raiders*. Atlanta: Mockingbird Books, 1956.

Keller, Allan. *Morgan's Raid*. New York: Collier Books, 1962.

Kirkland, Frazar. *The Pictorial Book of Anecdotes of the Rebellion*. St. Louis: J. H. Mason, 1889.

Lanier, Robert S. *The Photographic History of the Civil War*. Secaucus: The Blue and Grey Press, 1981.

McDonough, James Lee. *Chattanooga- A Death Grip on the Confederacy*. Knoxville: University of Tennessee Press, 1984.

McDonough, James Lee. *Shiloh- In Hell Before Night*. Knoxville: University of Tennessee Press, 1977.

McDonough, James Lee, and Thomas L. Connelly. *Five Tragic Hours: The Battle of Franklin*. Knoxville: University of Tennessee Press, 1984.

Miers, Earl S. *The Web of Victory: Grant at Vicksburg*. Baton Rouge: Louisiana State University Press, 1955.

Minnigh, L. W. *Gettysburg: What They Did Here*. Gettysburg: N. A. Meligakes, 1924.

Monaghan, Jay. *Civil War on the Western Border*. Boston: Little Brown and Company, 1955.

Phillips, Herb. *Champion Hill*. Champion Hill Battlefield Foundation, Inc., Edwards, 1986.

Piatt, D. *Men Who Saved the Union*. Mac-o-chee, 1887.

Pitkin, Thomas M. *Grant the Soldier*. Washington: Acropolis Books, 1965.

Pratt, Fletcher. *Ordeal By Fire*. New York: William Morrow & Co., Inc., 1948.

Pullen, John J. *The Twentieth Maine: A Volunteer Regiment in the Civil War*. Dayton: Morningside Bookshop, 1984.

Rhodes, Robert. *All For The Union: A History of the 2nd Rhode Island Volunteer Infantry in the War of the Great Rebellion*. Lincoln: Andrew Mowbray Incorporated, 1985.

Rich, Doris. *Fort Morgan and the Battle of Mobile Bay*. Foley: Underwood Printing Co., 1982.

Schott, Joseph L. *Action Above and Beyond*. New York: Popular Library, 1964.

Sears, Stephen W. *Landscape Turned Red: The Battle of Antietam.* New York: Warner Books, 1983.

Semmes, Raphael. *The Confederate Raider Alabama.* Greenwich: Fawcett Publications, 1962.

Siepel, Kevin H. *Rebel: The Life and Times of John Singleton Mosby.* New York: St. Martins Press, 1983.

Smith, Eugene O. *Lee and Grant: A Duel Biography.* New York: McGraw-Hill, 1984.

Smith, Howard K. *Washington, D.C.: The Story of Our Nation's Capital.* New York: Random House, 1967.

Stackpole, General Edward J. *They Met at Gettysburg.* Harrisburg: Stackpole Books, 1956.

Stampp, Kenneth M. *The Era of Reconstruction 1865–1877.* New York: Alfred A. Knopf, 1966.

Still, William N., Jr. *Iron Afloat: The Story of the Confederate Armorclads.* Columbia: University of South Carolina Press, 1985.

Straubing, Harold Elk. *The Fateful Lightning.* New York: Paragon House Publishers, 1985.

Swanberg, W. A. *First Blood: The Story of Fort Sumter.* New York: Charles Scribner's Sons, 1957.

Terdoslavich, William. *The Civil War Quiz Book.* New York: Warner Books, 1984.

Tucker, Glenn. *Chickamauga: Bloody Battle in the West.* Dayton: Morningside Bookshop, 1976.

Tucker, Glenn. *High Tide at Gettysburg.* Dayton: Morningside Bookshop, 1980.

Wheeler, Richard. *Sword Over Richmond: An Eyewitness History of McClellan's Peninsula Campaign.* New York: Harper & Row, 1986.

Williams, Edward F., III. *Confederate Victories at Fort Pillow.* Memphis: Nathan Bedford Forrest Trail Committee Historical Hiking Trails, Inc., 1984.

Woodward, W. E. *Meet General Grant.* New York: Liveright Publishing Corporation, 1928.